As You Were

As You Were

The Tragedy at Valcartier

GERRY FOSTATY

Edited by Paula Sarson.
Cover and page design by Julie Scriver.
Printed in Canada.
10 9 8 7 6 5 4 3 2 1

Library and Archives Canada Cataloguing in Publication

Fostaty, Gerry, 1956-
    As you were: the tragedy at Valcartier / Gerry Fostaty.

ISBN 978-0-86492-648-7

1. Fostaty, Gerry, 1956-.
2. Accident victims—Québec (Province)—Valcartier—Biography.
3. Military education—Accidents—Québec (Province)—Valcartier—History.
4. Explosions—Québec (Province)—Valcartier.
5. Canada. Canadian Forces Base (Valcartier, Québec). I. Title.

U442.A3F67 2011   355.5028'9   C2010-907054-2

Goose Lane Editions acknowledges the financial support of the Canada Council for the Arts, the Government of Canada through the Book Publishing Industry Development Program (BPIDP), and the New Brunswick Department of Wellness, Culture, and Sport for its publishing activities.

Goose Lane Editions
Suite 330, 500 Beaverbrook Court
Fredericton, New Brunswick
CANADA E3B 5X4
www.gooselane.com

Mixed Sources
Product group from well-managed forests,
controlled sources and recycled wood or fiber
www.fsc.org Cert no. SW-COC-000952
© 1996 Forest Stewardship Council
FSC

For Angie, Rosemary, Sam, and Ben, of course.

Contents

Preface

Altogether, my life has been no more interesting than anyone else's, but one extraordinary and horrible day has stayed with me for more than thirty years. In 1974, while I was on a cadet summer training assignment at Canadian Forces Base (CFB) Valcartier, a live grenade that somehow got mixed in among the teaching aids blew up during an indoor lecture on explosives safety. That day instantly changed me as only something terrible can. This story focuses on that day, although, for context, I touch on the days leading up to the incident and the few weeks that followed.

So, this is a memoir, a small slice that left an enduring impact on my life. I wasn't alone that day. More than one hundred and thirty others—mostly boys, some men—were with me, fifty or so of whom were as close to me as anyone can be who isn't family. I was with the group only a short time—with most just six weeks—and I admit with sadness and regret that I don't remember every one of them anymore. I recall the ones who made the biggest impression on me, though, whether positive or negative.

The names of the adults involved and the boys who were killed are a matter of public record, identified in the report of the official inquest made public by the Canadian Department of National Defence (DND) in 2006. Some parts of the story are not flattering; some of those I name might be embarrassed. But I have tried to represent everyone as I honestly remember them. In our youthfulness, we all were prone to impetuous, hotheaded, and energetic behaviour.

The scene of the story remains as I remember it. The cadet camp and the base where we trained in 1974, twenty-five kilometres north of Quebec City, sprawls northward from an area between the towns of Courcelette and Saint-Gabriel-de-Valcartier, the base's namesake. Cadets continue to train there in the summer, as they do at bases across Canada. Contrary to my usual inclination, when I came home at the end of August 1974, I wrote down all the events of that summer—every detail I could remember, trying to be as true to the facts as I could. Even at age eighteen, I knew it would be important to me one day.

The specifics of the story are drawn from the official DND records—mainly police reports, internal and external investigative reports, medical examiner's reports, internal communications, and the coroner's inquest that followed the incident. The details have been distilled through reading the many pages of documents readily obtainable from DND under the *Access to Information Act*. I have spent much time organizing the sequence of events and decisions that I did not witness but that preceded and ultimately led to the explosion and are detailed in the inquest.

This work is dedicated to the army cadets of D Company, CFB Valcartier, 1974—in particular, to the memory of those who died:

> Yves Langlois, age fifteen
> Pierre Leroux, age fourteen
> Eric Lloyd, age fourteen
> Othon Mangos, age fourteen
> Mario Provencher, age fifteen
> Michel Voisard, age fourteen

Fifty-four others were injured. Some of the survivors of that day walked away with invisible emotional injuries. They walked away alone. This memoir is also for them.

I wrote this book for two reasons. First, I never seemed to be able to tell the whole story in one go without interruption. It really is the kind of story that raises questions throughout, and the detours one must follow to answer them can assume a life of their own, prompting new questions and additional side trips. Although I have ventured to speak about that day to a few people, the questions they posed and the anger they exhibited before I could relate the whole story put me in the awkward position of sometimes defending policies and procedures I should have been condemning. I wanted to recount the story as it unfolded, in the hope that I could answer and even pre-empt some of those angry questions. Writing this book gave me the opportunity to organize the events and map everything on a timeline and to assemble the narrative in one place. I set the scene by describing the usual routines that occurred on a normal day of cadet summer training camp before the explosion.

The second reason I wrote the book is to tell my family what happened to me in 1974. My sisters and my mother surely had forgotten about it, while my children and my wife needed to know that something had changed my life thirty-four years ago — perhaps more important, *I* needed to tell them.

Some will disagree with my memories of that day. Some who were there might not recognize themselves in my account. All I can say is they stood where they stood, and I stood where I stood; our perspectives will naturally differ. This is how I remember it.

A cadet checks into the D Company OR on his first day.
Facing the cadet (from left to right) are Wheeler,
Fostaty, Katzko, and Fullum.

Were You There?

The name that appeared on my computer screen on February 14, 2008, was one I hadn't seen in thirty-four years. The sight of it in my email inbox sent a flush to my face and a chill down my spine. An adrenaline rush seemed to prompt me to stand or run as my mind flooded with memories of that day in 1974: the colour, olive drab; the smell of oiled canvas tents and boot polish; the noisy din of the mess; the grind of the mosquito-fogging truck as it wound its way through the base, trailing oily, bluish smoke behind it; the cadence of marching boot-shod feet and distant shouted commands. The memory of the sudden deep *crack* of the exploding grenade and breaking glass followed by screaming, the stinging reek of gunpowder and blood — there was so much blood.

The name was that of Charles Gutta. We struggle to remember people, events, and things in our lives, but I had no trouble remembering him. Even after all this time, the memory of him was as big as life. Not a tall man, but solid, in both his build and his demeanour. The lines on his fair face and the intensity of his gaze suggested an uncompromising nature, soon confirmed by his manner. I recalled that his salt-and-pepper brushcut hair belied his thirty-five or so years, but he had seemed old to me. I was eighteen then, when thirty-five seem aged; now I'm in my fifties, thirty-five seems like yesterday. Charles Gutta moved with purpose and economy and had no time for fools, as I painfully learned early in our acquaintance. He was no nonsense and no fluff. We quickly understood that Sergeant Charles Gutta was a man of his word, and his word was law.

I had thought that nothing would surprise me in an email anymore, but with the sudden appearance of this name on my computer I was clearly mistaken. His message was sitting in the middle of a pile of messages, but my eye was drawn to it in the same way one is compelled to look at something moving at the periphery of vision when all else is still.

The subject line was "Valcartier 1974." I almost didn't want to read the message. As I clicked the mouse to open it, I suddenly became aware of my heart beating, my breathing becoming shallow. The three-word message, like its author, got to the point: "Were you there?"

I had been there all right. I hit the reply button and began typing. "Yes. I have thought of you often. I hope you are well." Send.

I sat there looking at the screen, as if expecting that a reply would come back right away. I was baffled by what could have prompted him to contact me after all these years and how he had even remembered me. How had he found me? I sat there, transfixed by reminiscence.

By the summer of 1974, I had been a cadet for five years and had undergone the same training as the youths I would oversee were about to experience. The cadet movement, which traces its history back to 1879, is the oldest federally funded youth program in Canada. Although the movement is funded by and affiliated with the Canadian Forces, it is not technically part of the Forces. Cadets are not required to move on to regular or reserve service, though I'm sure every cadet at least thinks about it—I certainly did. The training I received at various summer camps and with my home unit had qualified me to apply to become a non-commissioned officer (NCO). I had advanced through the ranks and was certified as a cadet leader, senior cadet leader, and master cadet, and was now to become an NCO for the summertime cadet training at Valcartier.

Eventually, I pulled myself away from the computer and headed to my basement in search of some old boxes of memorabilia I had been dragging around with me for decades. These items had no practical value, and I would never use them again, but they were benchmarks of my life. Blowing the dust off one box, I dove in, looking for pictures from that summer I knew were there somewhere, though, of course, I couldn't find them right away.

Instead, I came across a small red leather journal, given to me in 1972 when I was training in Banff at the National Army Cadet Camp. Of Canada's twenty-five thousand or so army cadets, around two hundred and fifty were chosen each summer to take a six-week senior leadership course in Banff, and even then I realized how fortunate I was to have been invited. I had never been so far from my family before, and getting there was my first time on an airplane. I was sixteen.

I did not exactly excel at keeping a journal then, so within the red leather binding are just the addresses of a half-dozen or so British cadets I trained with that year. When they were finished with us, they were going off to the British Royal Military Academy at Sandhurst. Their home addresses had quaint names like Sifton House and Rose Hill. One fellow's home address was the British embassy in Prague; his father, apparently, was the military attaché. They were so different from us. We were loud and raw; they seemed sophisticated, polished, conservative, which for some of us made them a target for mockery.

That was the year Paul McCartney released "Give Ireland Back to the Irish." The record was on the canteen jukebox, and every time the Brits came in, someone would spend a quarter to play it. The Brits, of course, viewed this as bordering on treason. In retaliation, one would stand on another's shoulders, unhook the large photograph of Queen Elizabeth II from the wall, and together they would run out of the canteen with the picture, while a third Brit held the door open. They would stand outside until the song ended and then calmly re-hang the picture on the wall.

This pattern repeated over the course of a few days, until our commanding officer got wind of it. Instead of having the song removed from the jukebox, however, he forbade the Brits to remove the picture from the canteen. At first, they fumed and made a great show of disgust whenever the song played, which was annoyingly often. One day, however, they began to sit there smiling no matter how often the song came on, continuing to grin even when the canteen crowd loudly sang along. Eventually, the usual response not forthcoming, the jukebox became relatively quiet.

It was purely by chance that I discovered the reason for the Brits' newly relaxed attitude. I had arrived late and was looking for a place to sit when I spotted a few of my friends lounging at a table near the back wall. "Give Ireland Back to the Irish" was blaring on the jukebox. As I stepped around an overstuffed chair to sit down, I glanced up at the wall in front of me to see the picture of Her Majesty sporting the smallest of cotton balls, stuck to her ears. No one else had noticed, and I never said a word to anyone.

Whenever I see those addresses in the small red journal, I'm reminded of that story. Memory is fluid that way. One thing can link quickly to another, creating a string of memories just as in a treasure hunt where one clue leads to another.

I returned to the computer about an hour later to look at the message again, "Were you there?" and to reread my reply. Despite the initial shock of this contact out of the blue, I was glad Sergeant Gutta had sent the message. But as I anxiously awaited his response, I found myself lured down a path I did not really care to retread.

I don't remember saying goodbye to anyone when I left the base in 1974. I guess I just wanted to get home, to leave the explosion and the deaths and injuries and all that had happened far behind me. In retrospect, I suppose I thought home was the answer. Home implied stability and normality. Even at age eighteen, the irony was not lost on me that I had tried to get away from home for the same reasons I later wanted to return. I will see all these people from the base soon enough, I had thought. I was wrong, of course. Most of them I would never see again.

The young feel that the world and their relationships will remain as they leave them—like folding over the page of a novel and walking away, trusting the story will continue where we left off once we resume reading. I have learned, however, that, like reading a book, the longer you put aside a relationship, the more likely you will have to start at the beginning to make sense of it and regain continuity.

Over the years, I had often thought of the people I spent that summer with and wondered what became of them. I felt the occasional pull to contact them, but how would I begin what might be a one-sided conversation with someone I hadn't seen in years? Would I be remembered? Would they want to be contacted? Could I reach the right people just by pulling names out of the phone book? In the days before email or even telephone answering machines, it would have been just me, a phone book, and the electric hum of a dial tone prompting me to dial. In the end, I was too timid to make any calls. What held us together was the horror of the explosion, but it was both a bond and a barrier.

Searching

For a few years after 1974, the survivors with whom I had briefly come in contact avoided any talk of the explosion or communication with anyone who had been there. I imagine, for them as for me, that summer was like a shadowy underwater spectre, usually hidden deep below but surfacing occasionally and briefly. At times, I wanted very much to talk about that day, but what could I say to someone who hadn't been there? How could I possibly raise the subject in a conversation?

Even in talking about it to my wife, my words fell thin and flat, reflecting none of the frenzy and the horror and the ache that remained. When I made even a sidelong reference to it, though, she would look at me as though I were breakable. I am not breakable. Perhaps I was afraid to admit weakness and to yield to it. Perhaps, too, I couldn't find adequate words to express my feelings, I feared I would sound clichéd, false, perhaps trivializing the event and dishonouring the memory of those we lost. The friends I returned home to in 1974 never knew, and new friends never learned of it.

My brother Nick, four years my junior, was with me that summer, and for a few horrifying minutes I thought I had lost him forever. Nick had decided to become a cadet as well. He was advancing quickly and had won himself a spot at CFB Valcartier. After we returned home, he became withdrawn for a time, and in his own silent grieving he often sat alone, staring into the distance. He refused to speak about the explosion, and became angry and even abusive if I pressed him. He didn't realize that I needed his support as much as he chose not to need mine.

Nick had taken to wearing a token of that summer around his neck, under his shirt: a picture of a friend he had lost. He had tied it there with a string too short to be pulled back over his head and wetted the knot tight. When I asked him why he wore it, he said he was afraid he would forget.

Sometime in late September, about a month after we got home, I managed to sit down with him. In his face I read anger because he supposed I was about to confront him. I wasn't there to battle with him, though, but to rescue him from his self-imposed prison. It wasn't an act of altruism, either. I felt he was my responsibility, as were the others in my platoon, and his pain and grief were directly tied to my feeling of having failed to protect him, and them.

I sat across from him. We were alone. I didn't say a word but just passed him some scissors. He knew what I meant because that string around his neck had become his focus. But he cut the string, and cried. He still refused to speak about it, though, and when he died years later, there was no longer even a promise of someone for me to talk to.

As the years sped by, it became more and more difficult to contact my old friends. People moved, and I lost any hope of reconnecting with them. I realized I had assumed they would always be there, just safely over the horizon, but, like a neglected garden, I let them go. The path back to these relationships soon became overgrown with the weeds of inattention. It seemed impossible that I would find it again.

Rare chance meetings were seized before they vanished. One such opportunity arose in 2007. I was at the airport in Vancouver, waiting at the gate for a flight to Calgary. Had I arrived a minute earlier or later, I might have chosen another seat facing in another direction and not seen him at all. But a seat became free just as I entered the waiting area, and I sat down. It was crowded, and I swung my briefcase behind my legs to keep it from under peoples' feet. When I looked up, I was surprised to see Vince Muolo standing in line. We had spent two years in training together and then another year as NCOs in H Company at CFB Valcartier Cadet Camp in 1973. I hadn't seen him in more than thirty years, but I was sure it was him. I was amazed at how little he had changed. Remarkably, he still looked almost as young as I remembered him. There was not even a touch of grey in his hair. I watched from my seat as he got into line when they called the flight, and he disappeared down the Jetway. I would be boarding that plane, too, so there was still an opportunity.

I knew if I didn't say hello to him I would always regret it. As I made my way down the aisle to my seat, behind people dragging bags and holding children, I watched him as he threw his carry-on bag into an overhead bin. I found my seat, on the aisle, jammed my laptop bag under the seat in front of me, and, after the crowd had thinned out, tentatively made my way back to his spot. He was putting a briefcase under the seat as I cautiously said, "Vince?"

"Yes?" he said, straightening up and looking at me quizzically. Then he smiled and blurted out, "My God!" I was shocked and pleased that after thirty years he would remember me. We talked for a bit and exchanged wide-eyed, astonished looks and then email addresses before we were bidden back to our seats for takeoff. We spoke a bit again during the forty-five minute flight. I was staying in Calgary, where we landed, but he was getting on a connecting flight to Ottawa. We exchanged a few polite emails thereafter, but we lost touch again. Those weeds of inattention quickly grew over our line of communication. We really were strangers.

That chance meeting with Vince started me thinking anew about what had happened in 1974 and to the others I had trained and worked with as a cadet. Although Vince hadn't been with me when the grenade exploded, he had trained with me the three previous summers and would have known many of D Company. Meeting Vince, however, gave me the courage to approach other old friends from 1974 if the chance ever arose.

The next opportunity presented itself in the form of the message from Sergeant Gutta. And while I felt a bit uneasy, I was determined to seize it with both hands.

A few years before Sergeant Gutta contacted me, I had come across my regimental cap badge and uniform name tag while cleaning out a drawer. I had stared at these fragments—the only evidence connecting me to the most horrible time in my life. I also had my memories, of course, which I revisited all too frequently, but nothing else. I started to wonder then if I could find any information about that summer. The press had largely ignored the explosion at the time except for the tabloid *Le Journal de Montréal,* which ran a screaming headline, "Massacre à Valcartier," the day after it happened. Subsequent press mentions, however, seemed brief and well-buried: I recalled there had been a small article in the middle of the *Toronto Star* some months later that outlined the results of the subsequent civilian coroner's inquest.

I also began searching the Internet for any scrap of information about the explosion and turned up a few mildly disturbing references. One appeared as a fiery response to a letter to the editor in 2008 in the on-line *Globe and Mail* from someone who claimed to have been there. He was using what he deemed his close association with the incident to boost his credibility as the contributor of an article in support of the troops in Afghanistan. He said he understood what the troops were going through because some of his fellow cadets had died at Valcartier in 1974. I was shocked. He might have been at the base on the other side of the camp, but his claim of involvement was purely illusory. I was angry and hurt, and I felt a sense of violation that someone would lie about being there. He was an anglophone, and all the anglos had been in my platoon. He revealed further into his letter that he had been in another company, on exchange from another province.

Any real press coverage, I thought, must have disappeared into the newspapers' archives, but most had not been digitally captured at the time I searched, and those that existed generally went only as far back as 2000. That would mean searching through back issues at the newspaper offices or scrolling through microfilm at the library. I would get to that in time, I thought.

The only other mentions of the explosion I found on the Internet were in a few chat forums. One or two had incorrect information, another suggested the explosion was some sort of urban legend or myth. I did find something in a forum on the Black Watch regimental

Web site in 2006 that was sympathetic, although largely uninformed. The first posting was dated 2004. I posted an anonymous message in response to the kind things that had been said about the people who had been there. It seemed quite a few people posting messages on that site about the summer of 1974 felt they knew someone who knew someone who had been there.

There was also some scepticism about the incident, so I jumped into the conversation. I felt obliged to let them know, at least anonymously, that it really did happen. I didn't want to reveal who I was, though. I remember typing and deleting the message numerous times, my hands shaking. There was no reason for it, really; it had all happened so long ago. When I finally hit the "post" button, my hand trembling on the mouse, I understood I had been affected by the memories of that summer much more than I realized. Occasionally, I went back to the Black Watch Web site and found a few others like me, almost all of whom used pseudonyms to guard their anonymity. Then, one day, I looked in on the site to find the Webmaster had posted a note proudly announcing a new design and stating that all the old postings had been deleted—our conversations were erased. Not only was our contact now broken, there was no longer a landing page for the Internet search engines to index, so there would be an even smaller chance of finding one another again.

Can You Attend?

Mornings have always come too quickly for my taste, and the morning of February 15, 2008, was no exception. I was startled awake by the sound of voices on the all-news radio station on the bedside radio alarm. With the reflexes of a cat I hit the snooze bar. Although my wife also gets up for work at the same time as me every morning, I feel it is my duty to shield her from the unapologetic traffic and weather report that blasts from the radio when the alarm goes off. I am not fool enough to think she can't hear it, but it is important to me that she knows I am thinking of her.

As a teenager, I used to set my big red clock radio almost to the maximum volume as I found that, at a lower level, I would sleep through the alarm. Well, to be fair, my father made this discovery. He worked nights, and on the mornings when I slept through the alarm, he would storm into my room and growl at me to get out of bed and shut off the music. So, I learned to set the volume very loud and to position the radio across the room to launch me out of bed before my father had a chance to react. I don't set the volume high anymore, but I do still pounce on the alarm.

This morning, instead of drifting back to sleep as usual, I lay awake, exhausted, my heart pounding. The alarm had jolted me awake like an electric shock. I stared at the ceiling, occasionally turning my head to look at the clock, waiting for it to come to life again. With a minute to go, I turned it off. Defeated, I rolled out of bed and headed to the kitchen to start my morning routine.

The first order of business is always to put on the coffee. This morning, though, I switched on the computer first to let it boot up while I got breakfast ready and headed outside to get the paper. The paper was late, so with my coffee in hand I checked my email. Another message from Charles Gutta! Until yesterday, when I received his first note, I had not even known his first name—he was just Sergeant Gutta, our company sergeant major.

"There will be a memorial on the 31st of July at 1000 hours at the base. Would it be possible for you to attend?" He still got straight to the point, as I remembered him. His message continued, "I would like to contact all the members from our time for the thirty-fifth anniversary. This year, 2008, a meet and greet. I am in contact with the following members. [He named three others.] Where are you writing from and do you have any contact with any members from D Company? Please do not break this contact."

There was a sense of urgency in his last sentence, but then I remembered he had a way of giving weight to everything he said. He had the kind of delivery that truly commanded attention. "Porte attention! Listen up!" he would bark, and the area would go silent.

I couldn't say no. You don't say no to your company sergeant major, and frankly, even after thirty-four years, I didn't want to. I could almost hear his voice delivering the request. I smiled as I thought, if he were here, he would repeat it in French. He always seemed to begin with the language that reflected the majority of the people standing before him, and then he would repeat it in the second language for the minority. I could never discern what his first language was. He spoke both English and French equally well, although the formality of his phrasing and the precision of his consonants made me suspect there was at least a third language in his arsenal.

As I sat at the computer, another message popped up, and a wave of adrenaline shot through me. Yvan Fullum! He had been our company clerk—Sergeant Gutta evidently had passed my contact info on to him—and he had attached a picture to his greeting. It was a photo of the platoon. I had trouble seeing it at first—the old black-and-white

10 Platoon after the explosion.

picture had been scanned at a low resolution and appeared grainy and sideways on my screen. I quickly captured it, rotated it, and enhanced it with some graphics software to get a better look.

There we were: some standing, some sitting in front of the clutch of trees that stood across the road from the company. We were all smiling. My God, we were young. There were the company officers, front and centre, seated on a long wooden bench. Aleth Bruce, a corporal from my platoon, was beside me on the left; on the opposite side of the officers stood the other corporals, Karl Medvescek, Glenn Souva, and, crouched down, Yvan Fullum. The rest of the platoon stood behind the officers, the first row on the ground and the second row on a wooden bench at the back. Something was wrong, though. I did a head count:

twenty-nine. But there had been forty-seven in the platoon. Then I remembered: we'd had a second picture taken after the explosion. The first picture was never released to us. It was as if those missing had never been there. I wondered if my smile somehow betrayed those who were missing.

The picture, I realized, is symptomatic of the way the events of that summer had been treated: with active disregard and the hope they would all go away quietly. They did, too. It seemed no one remembered what had happened but those who were there. No one counselled us then, and it seemed we were still keeping everything to ourselves. Nowadays, there would be counselling and emotional support from a post-trauma stress team and probably a Royal Commission. On October 10, 2008, I heard on the news while on my way to work that there had been two accidental deaths the day before during a training exercise at CFB Moose Jaw. The commanding officer, Colonel Paul Keddy, was being interviewed and was letting the press and public know that counselling was under way for all base personnel, their families, and the families of the victims. On the day of the accident itself, the *Toronto Star* reported Colonel Keddy as saying, "The members of 15 Wing have come together over the last several hours to respond to this, keeping in mind the needs of the families."[1]

It was different for us back in 1974. No one asked us how we were doing, either at the time or later. When it was all over, we went our separate ways. There was no need for a support group because there was no longer any group.

So I was surprised to learn from Sergeant Gutta's email that a small memorial was held every year at the base. It was a well-kept secret, that annual memorial. I had never been invited. Who was it for, and who attended, if not those who had been there? My reaction was to accept the sergeant's invitation for now, and then think about it over the next four months. I didn't want to be a back-row spectator at the memorial, not when I'd had a ringside seat at the main event. Had others from D Company been there? Had I missed chances to meet them again? Had the families of those who had died been invited to the memorials all these years? Or would this be the first time any of us would be there? I was consumed by questions.

Curiosity got the better of me, and I began poking around on the Internet again looking for a few of the people I could remember. I started with those who had unusual names, as they would be the easiest to find, and came across a few, although none with direct contact information. I would have to take a roundabout approach, and decided I would leave that for later.

I then started searching for archived news items on the explosion, this time using different combinations of keywords and synonyms. It looked as though Sergeant Gutta had been looking for members of D Company, too, as I found he had posted the same message on military forums all over the place, presumably in the hope that it would be seen and answered. Evidently, my keywords were matching his forum posts, but I adjusted my search terms and kept looking.

Almost immediately, I had a hit on a government Web site. As a part of the *Access to Information Act*, DND had announced the release of "All documentation related to the explosion on the Valcartier Cadet Base 31 July 1974, to include the following types of reports: internal/external, investigative, recommendation, coroner and medical examiner, governmental as well as media reports."[2] Moreover, it was available to anyone who requested it.

I hoped that "investigative" meant they would include the information and findings of the civilian inquest that had followed. There had also been an investigation at the base by the Military Police and the Sûreté du Québec. Along with a military board of inquiry on the base, during which I had been questioned, and a coroner's inquest followed by a civil trial, that would add up to a lot of information, if it was all included.

I was stunned by the luck of my find, and quickly downloaded and filled out the application form. I wrote a cheque for the fee and put everything in an envelope, which I shoved in my pocket. I felt it was a bold step to ask for all the information; it might shine a light on facts better left in the dark. But could some written facts be any worse than what we saw that day? I popped the envelope into the first mailbox I came across on my way to work. I was sure it would be months before I heard anything from DND.

It wasn't months, though, but a mere three weeks before a package arrived: a large padded manila envelope emblazoned with "Department of National Defence Access to Information and Privacy" and a notice of expedited delivery. I laid it on the kitchen table apart from the rest of the mail and went to wash my hands in the sink.

"What's that?" asked my wife as she blew into the kitchen, her arms full of paperwork and a gym bag over her shoulder. She freed up a hand by clutching the paperwork under her chin and picked up the envelope to read aloud, "Department of National Defence." She held it out to me as I dried my hands. It had made as much of an impact on her as a brochure from a lawn care company.

"It must be the final report of the inquiry," I said, taking it. She breezed out of the room with a disinterested, "Ah...," swung the gym bag down to the floor in the hall, and continued into another room to drop off her paperwork.

My sons didn't even notice the envelope. A letter from DND would have attracted *my* interest no matter whom it had been addressed to, so it seemed strange to me that my family had paid no attention to it. Undaunted by their indifference to an official letter from the government, I put the envelope back on the table with much dignity, not because of its origins but because I was convinced the report inside would shine a spotlight on information that was missing from my experiences during that summer of 1974.

We had dinner and went through the usual evening family routine, shuttling my sons here and there to their after-school activities and getting homework done, before I could settle down to the envelope. I felt I had shown remarkable restraint by leaving it until I could focus on it, but now I wanted to give it my full attention. I began by reading everything there was to read on the outside of the envelope. Then I carefully opened it.

I had thought that the package, when it arrived, would be thick and heavy with documents, but on inspecting it now, I realized it was neither thick nor heavy. I looked inside to find only a single sheet of paper. I was sure this would be a note telling me I was not entitled to the report, and I was about to be outraged by the waste of putting a single sheet of paper in such a huge padded envelope. The note, however, informed me that the full report was enclosed. Surely, I thought, someone has forgotten to include it. I reached inside once more, though, and discovered a CD jewel case: electronic copies!

I flipped the jewel case open to reveal a plain CD with the report number handwritten on it with a Sharpie. I hurried to my computer and slid the CD into the drive. It whirred and spun to reveal eleven Acrobat files. I opened the first file and rapidly scrolled through the pages. Then I went through all the others the same way to get a feel for what was there. There was no introduction on any of the files, no summary, and no conclusion or recommendation, just the inquest data arranged in no particular order—sheets and sheets scanned and digitized.

What struck me at first was that most of the documents were typewritten—not the neat, justified text, and proportionally spaced lettering of word-processed pages we are used to now, but the stained and unevenly typed pages of thirty years ago, with clunky-looking, mono-spaced letters in Courier typescript. Some of the typewriter keys had been out of alignment and some of the letters must have been clogged with dirt, so that an *e* sometimes looked like an *o*. Some spelling mistakes had been left alone, others had been scratched out with a pen and corrected by hand. There was no evidence of correction fluid, either. Where a mistake had been made, the typist had simply obliterated the error with *x*'s. "Confidential," in capital letters, had been rubber-stamped at the top and bottom of every page. The heading "Unclassified without attachment" was sprinkled throughout, meaning the documents were no longer classified.

Some pages contained handwritten notes, accompanied by rubber-stamped dates and the signatures and initials of those who had read the report as it made its way through the Military Police, Sûreté du Québec, and National Defence Headquarters. Crumples and creases picked up during the photocopying process showed that the documents had been well handled, if not handled well. There were handwritten declarations, as well—penned, signed, and initialled by those who had had a hand in our destiny weeks before that summer day in 1974.

I scanned the documents greedily and took them in gulps at first. Because the files had been assembled in no particular order, the chronology hopped around. The events had been laid down in the order in which the police collected information when they interviewed witnesses, so I had my work cut out for me to establish the sequence of events preceding the explosion. I was surprised and reassured that the personal accounts in the report didn't change anything that I remembered from that day. Gradually, the documents filled in for me why and how the incident had happened.

A trail of related events occurred over a two-week period preceding the explosion: errors of both omission and commission that snaked their way back and forth through people and places. These errors could have been corrected at several points, but they weren't. As I read, I was reminded of something a friend told me, "Take care of the little things and the large things take care of themselves." I couldn't help thinking that, if people had understood how their responsibilities and actions would reach beyond their own immediate sphere of sight and touch, they might have taken greater care of what had been entrusted to them.

I read the documents with a sense of dread as I followed the path of the deadly grenade to its final destination. I read knowing the terrifying outcome, but I still hoped that something would change its course. It took days and days of reading and rereading to find out exactly what had happened. There were so many types of documents—not just police and coroner's reports and interviews with witnesses, but inventory sheets from the ammunition depot, a map of the room showing where everyone sat, hospital reports of the injuries of the survivors, ammunition movement and tonnage reports, and handwritten testimonies, among others. I had to stop many times to look back at previous pages or to read the testimony of two or three people side by side to piece the puzzle together.

There were times, too, when I found myself unable to continue reading, my hands up to my mouth and my eyes full of tears, as I sat with the coroner's report on the screen in front of me. It wasn't that I was surprised to read about the boys' deaths, but I wasn't prepared for the way the clinical descriptions of the causes of death assaulted me. Knowing that someone died in an explosion is one thing, but learning that the cause of death was "cerebral lacerations by projectiles, metal and bone fragments"[3] seemed to slow the action down so that one could almost imagine the tiny bits of metal and pieces of bone tearing flesh as the victim's life drained from him.

It was difficult and emotionally charged work, but I was trying to find my way back through the testimony and events to where it all began, laying the facts down, one at a time like interlocking stones, to create a pathway. It all began, as so many misfortunes do, with the best of intentions.

Lecture Preparations

At the beginning of July 1974, Captain Jean-Claude Giroux, the commanding officer of the Ammunition Section at CFB Valcartier, was asked by the Cadet Camp to lecture the cadets who would be there for summer training on the security of explosives. "He was responsible for the storage, the receipt, the issue, and the technical supervision of the munitions for Base Valcartier and Eastern Quebec, as well as for the disposal of the explosives."[4] Although he didn't generally give lectures, Captain Giroux's expertise and position made him eminently suited to the task. An army base could have unexploded ordnance in unlikely spots, so the lectures were intended to ensure that no one got hurt by exploring something they thought, in their limited experience, was inert or just a harmless curiosity. Others on Captain Giroux's team were qualified as well, and so he detailed one, Warrant Officer Gaetan Campeau, who had been working in ammunition depots for nineteen years, to give the lectures. Campeau, in fact, had given the lectures the year before.[5]

On the morning of July 15, 1974, Campeau organized the display items and dummy explosives he would use in the explosives safety lecture. His selection purposefully reflected a wide range of ordnance, including grenades, anti-personnel mines, and rockets. He told the police investigators that he first went to building #38 to fetch a booby trap and a G-4 mine (mechanism); secondly he went to building TDM number 6 to take various items, of which a 36M sectioned grenade, a 3 inch sectioned mortar, a cannon bullet, a 2 inch body of empty mortar, a 81MM display smoke, a 3.5 rocket dummy, a sectioned MT rocket, a 60MM display representing a HE, a P.I.A.T. dummy and maybe some others. Thirdly, he went to building #115 to take two M-61 grenades in two containers, two 36M grenades, an anti-tank dummy mine, a C-17 display rocket, an 84mm dummy, and a 66MM-M62 dummy launcher and some other items.[6]

All of them were painted bright colours and marked to distinguish them from the live models. There was no guessing with these — the gaudy colours and markings let personnel know at a glance that these were dummies. Live explosives were olive green.

Campeau's first lecture of cadets was delivered at F Company on July 15 at 1330. After the lecture, he personally stored the dummy items at the ammunition depot in building #22. The next day at 0830, he lectured A Company;[7] afterward, he returned to the ammunition depot in the same khaki truck he had used to transport the lecture dummies, and asked Gérard Drolet, an employee at the ammunition depot, to empty the truck and place the dummies in safety.[8] For reasons unnamed in the testimonies, the request wasn't met at the time, and the dummies sat in the back of the truck for two more days.

Two days later, on July 18 at 0830, Corporal Claude Daoust of the Combat Arms School at CFB Valcartier went to the ammunition depot and took possession of 160 live M-61 grenades to bring them to the Combat Arms School quartermaster. They were to be used in grenade-throwing instruction. The M-61 grenade is a fragmentation hand grenade. It is lemon shaped and has a coil of notched steel covered with a smooth, thin, steel layer. Within the coil is an explosive centre. When detonated, the core shatters the coil and the steel casing, transforming the broken particles into high-velocity, irregularly shaped projectiles that can cause casualties up to fifteen metres away. It is a very effective anti-personnel device. That is, it was designed to kill and injure soldiers or anyone within its effective range. Because of its effectiveness, the design has been widely copied by many nations.

The M-61 grenades were ready for Corporal Daoust when he arrived—one hundred fifty sat in five wooden boxes, thirty to a box, and the remaining ten were in a cardboard box.[9] Daoust signed the requisition, mistakenly putting the date as July 17, copying what Gérard Drolet had already incorrectly written on the form.[10] Daoust drove the grenades over to the Combat Arms School quartermaster and handed them off to the weapons instructor, Sergeant Albert Doucet.

In training that morning, the Combat Arms School used all but nineteen of the grenades, and at about 1130 these were ready to be returned to the ammunition depot. Sergeant Doucet counted the grenades, placed them in a wooden box, and handed it off to Sergeant Eddy Leroux from the school quartermaster for the trip back to the depot.[11] Leroux testified that the grenades were in their cylindrical fibreboard containers. Ordinarily, adhesive tape would be on the containers and pieces of Styrofoam would stabilize the grenades within the canisters, but these had been removed at the practice range. Leroux, in fact, wasn't sure if the Styrofoam pieces were missing, even though he opened all of them.[12] "These grenades were all to be used. However, during the course, one grenade didn't explode and in that case dynamite had to be used to make it explode, which took about forty-five minutes."[13] The extra time used to detonate the faulty grenade meant they had run out of time for instruction, and consequently, they had not used all the grenades.

By 1145, Corporal Daoust had driven the remaining nineteen grenades in the wooden box in the rear of the truck back to the ammunition depot. He testified that he had wanted to return the grenades before lunch, so they wouldn't be lying around.[14] At the depot, Daoust once again met Drolet, the depot employee who had released the live grenades that morning. Drolet counted the grenades to verify the number, signed for them, and asked Daoust to place them, in their wooden box, in the rear box of a khaki-coloured truck belonging to the ammunition depot. "Because the area was under repair (asphalt), the exchanges were made behind the truck."[15]

The box of the truck was covered with a canvas, which Drolet held up to allow Daoust to place the wooden box of grenades in the back. Daoust picked up the wooden box, making sure it was closed properly, and lifted it into the truck. As he did so, he noticed articles lying about on the truck floor, but couldn't really identify them.

Daoust didn't know it, but this was the same truck—#73-20656—that Warrant Officer Campeau had used to transport the dummy grenades for his explosives safety lecture two days earlier,[16] and the dummies were still lying there.

It was almost lunchtime, so Drolet signed the requisition with the notation "subject to check," and left the cargo of live grenades in the truck, intending to deal with them after lunch. For reasons not specified in the testimonies—whether he was preoccupied, distracted, or got called away—Drolet forgot about the grenades until 1600 that afternoon. Then, he mentioned to Jean-Paul Poire, another employee of the ammunition depot, that some live grenades had come back earlier that day and that he had placed them in the back of the truck. Warrant Officer Campeau, who was nearby and had overheard some part of this exchange, asked Drolet where the grenades were. Drolet confirmed they were still in the khaki truck. Campeau then "compelled Drolet to take it out because he didn't want any grenade there."[17]

Upon reaching the truck and uncovering the box, Drolet found that the live grenades were now in a cardboard box, but he didn't remember moving them from the wooden box in which they had been originally.[18] As Drolet and Poire started to carry the box away from the truck, Campeau stopped them and then quickly checked the back of the truck. There, he found that a live grenade had fallen from the cardboard box and lay among the dummies. He removed the grenade from the truck and handed it to Drolet. He checked around further, but did not turn up any others. "WO CAMPEAU Gaetan asked Drolet if they had all the grenades and the latter answered positively."[19]

He was mistaken: another live M-61 grenade sat among the dummies in the back of the truck. Testimony later revealed that an empty fibre grenade canister was found at the scene of the explosion. That canister was identified as having come from the same lot as the eighteen live grenades from the back of the truck.[20]

Campeau told Drolet to take the live grenades to building #22, which served as a transit for all locations on the base regarding the issue and receipt of ammunition. When Drolet arrived at building #22, he realized he had forgotten the keys to get in. Poire, who was helping Drolet carry the box of grenades, testified that he told Drolet, as it was toward the end of the day, "we'll place them in the guardroom, that is building #36. I have a room that locks."[21] So Drolet and Poire took the live grenades to building #36, a guardroom near the gate of the ammunition depot, locked them in the cleaning room, and went home. Drolet came to work the next day, but reportedly forgot all about the grenades in the cleaning room of building #36. Poire couldn't remind him of them, either—he had gone on vacation.

The next day, July 19, immediately following the morning coffee break, Warrant Officer Campeau asked Roland Fournel and René Allaire, two employees of the ammunition depot, to remove the dummies from the truck because he wanted to use it later on that afternoon. In the truck, however, they found all the dummies lying around loose instead of in a box, as they had been when they were returned.

By then it had started to rain quite heavily, so Fournel and Allaire quickly put together a cardboard box and gathered the items into it. Allaire noticed "that there were M-36 and M-61 grenades in containers, but he didn't take care, since they were all supposed to be dummies."[22] They didn't check the items because it was raining and there were no documents to check them against. They then took the dummy grenades—and the one live grenade of which they were unaware—to building #22 and placed the box on the floor by the door. The box would remain there until it was needed again for the next two lectures on July 23 and July 30.[23]

Testimonies recount that, on the afternoon of July 19, Warrant Officer Campeau, who was about to go on vacation, had a conversation with Captain Giroux about taking over the explosives safety lectures to the cadets. "There was no written procedure to give the course,"[24] but Campeau advised Giroux about the lecture he should give. "It is very simple," said Campeau. "Don't turn around. Three words."[25]

He explained the process he used to teach the course. First, he would have all the cadets sit in a semicircle. Then he would take the items out of the box one by one, describe each one, and place it on the table. He would make it clear to the cadets why unexploded items sometimes might be found on the ranges. He told Giroux to check the items before the lecture and then again in front of the cadets. "Make sure to explain to them that most of the colours they see are not the right colours,"[26] referring to the fact that live grenades were dark green and dummies were painted brighter colours. If a cadet saw an object that looked like a dummy but was painted green, he should not touch it but report it.

With Warrant Officer Campeau on vacation, Captain Giroux delivered the safety lecture as planned to C Company at the cadet camp on July 23 at 1330, having been driven there by Corporal Jacques Cadieux, a supply technician who had worked at the ammunition depot for about a year.

> The lecture was given outside for about one hundred and thirty cadets. He listened to the lecture because the captain had asked him to stay with him. The captain presented a history of ammunitions, he explained the operation of the items and then the cadets came to look at those items and had them circulated. At one time, he saw a cadet who took a grenade from a container. Cpl CADIEUX Jacques noticed the number 6880 on the container. He immediately went forward to take it off the hands of the young cadet, for according to him, the number attracted his attention. He took the container in his hands and

replaced it in the cardboard box. The reason why he did that was that he believed there were enough grenades which were circulated amongst the young people.[27]

Cadieux reported to the Military Police investigators that he believed he had seen a small piece of Styrofoam when the cadet opened the container. In his report, the investigator wrote, "At the end of the lecture, [Cadieux] gathered all the items and went to place the box in the transit. He remembered that the grenades which were circulated amongst the cadets that day were replaced in the cardboard box, but not in their containers."[28]

The live grenades, which had been returned from the grenade practice range on July 18 and placed in the cleaning room of building #36 by Drolet and Poire, would stay where they were, forgotten, until July 31 or August 1, some days after the explosion, when Poire received an urgent phone call from Sergeant Albanie Pitre, who worked at the ammunition depot.[29] When the live grenades were retrieved from the cleaning room, they were recounted: there were only eighteen—one was missing. According to testimonies, no one would notice the difference until a day or two after the explosion, when Jean-Paul Poire walked into the cleaning room and discovered the box of grenades.[30]

Pre-inspection

Memory can be selective. It is too easy to shine a light on the high points, to create a "greatest hits" version of our lives. Thirty-four years have a way of softening and refracting that light, but this day remains crystal clear to me from the moment I woke up. Not only did I have an unwavering regimental routine to rely upon, but I had also written everything down soon after the fact, to have a record if needed someday.

That summer at CFB Valcartier, I took an oath:

> I do swear, that I will be faithful and bear true allegiance
> to Her Majesty, Queen Elizabeth the Second, Queen of
> Canada, Her heirs and successors according to law.
> So help me God.[31]

That is how my service began, and I meant every word.

•

As I opened my eyes on Tuesday, July 30, 1974, I automatically brought my arm up to see my watch. It was only 0430, and I was entitled to a half-hour more sleep, so I closed my eyes. I and the other NCOs of the company rose every morning an hour before the cadets. On an army base, time is important. There is always somewhere you have to be, and you always have to be there on time. As a cadet, I had waited for someone to tell me where to be and what to do, but I was a sergeant now, and my job was to make sure that everyone in my platoon was where they should be. Although I was technically still a cadet at my home unit and not officially a part of the Canadian Armed Forces, here at CFB Valcartier, I was an ex-cadet, a reservist, and officially employed by DND to train cadets on a leadership course.

The previous summer, I had been a corporal at H Company and had seen three groups of junior cadets throughout the period. This summer I would have just one group for the entire six-week period. I had arrived with the other NCOs in June, about two weeks ahead of the cadets, to go through an orientation, get sorted into companies or other assignments, trained in the specifics of our duties, and then prepare for the cadets' arrival in the first week of July. We could be posted to all kinds of assignments: jobs in the kitchen, as drivers, letter carriers (which we called postées), lifeguards, sports instructors, photographers, support staff, and, of course, working with the cadets in the companies. That was what I preferred, and I considered working in D Company the plum job since I had been a cadet in the same company a few years before.

The cadets in our D Company were between fourteen and seventeen years old. They had been chosen by their cadet corps as a reward for their hard work and dedication and invited to participate here at the camp. There was no cost to the cadets to participate: the Canadian Forces would cover transportation to the camp, food, lodging, uniforms, and all aspects of the training. The cadets even received a bonus of one hundred dollars for attending. But this was no summer camp for privileged, rich suburbanites; it was a camp embedded in an army base, steeped in military tradition and discipline, teaching real-life skills with military precision. The cadets would work together, play together, eat together, sleep under the same roof, and arise at the same time.

The next time I opened my eyes, I didn't have to look at my watch. It was obviously time to get the day under way. The lights were on and some of the other guys were already up, half-dressed, groggy, and quietly folding their bedding. I rubbed the sleep from my eyes, sat up, and looked around, wondering what the hell I was doing here. I sat there for a moment squinting, trying to get accustomed to the bright light. I was on a top bunk and very close to the bare bulb that hung from the ceiling, burning its two hundred watts only a few metres away from me. Most people were still asleep at this hour. I glanced at my watch—0502. I looked toward the window and saw it was still dark outside. A large cluster of trees just outside the window obscured our view of the sky anyway, so even if the sky was beginning to lighten, it would still look dark out there for a while.

The usual time for reveille was 0530, but the camp commander, Colonel Robert Whitelaw, would be making an inspection tour of our company that morning, so we had to get an early start at cleaning, prepping, and polishing. Everything had to be perfectly in order. We had been informed the day before that the colonel was quite partial to our company and that we were to keep it that way. Colonel Whitelaw had been our company commander for a few years, including the year that I had first come here as a cadet in 1971. Every year, D Company had won the annual award for best company while he commanded it, and we were to carry on the tradition now that he was the camp commanding officer (CO).

There were fourteen of us here in the NCOs' quarters: fourteen bunks in a six-by-six-metre room. We were the lowest-level instructors but an important cog in the machinery of the cadet camp. We were the corporals and sergeants of D Company. Our job, in the simplest terms, was to get the forty or so cadets in each platoon where they needed to be and to assist with the training as well as maintain order and discipline. Besides the corporals of my 10 Platoon, Karl Medvescek, Glenn Souva, and Aleth Bruce, and our company clerk Yvan (Bubbles) Fullum, there were André Joannic, Jocelyn Desmeules, and Serge Plante, the corporals of 11 Platoon, and Paul Wheeler, Tony Snopek, Mark Slater, and Bahadur Banzal, the corporals of 12 Platoon. Bob Gibeault, Daniel (Moose) Seguin, and I were the platoon sergeants.

Bob Gibeault, the sergeant of 11 Platoon, was tall and slim and had an easygoing way about him. Nothing seemed to irritate him. His leadership style was direct and brief. I once saw a cadet question his request. Bob looked at him and said, "Are you through?"

"Yes, Sergeant."

"Good," said Bob in an even tone. "Now do as I told you."

"Yes, Sergeant," said the cadet, who hurried to comply.

Moose Seguin was the sergeant of 12 Platoon. He was shorter than Gibeault and he was solidly built. Although he looked tough, he was very friendly. No one on parade would guess, though, because his voice changed to a growl, and he sneered while giving drill commands.

I was the second-in-command of 10 Platoon. I was skinny, relying on my uniform to fill me out, and I had a light voice. I was completely the opposite of what you might expect in a sergeant. My platoon commander was Lieutenant Gary Katzko, who had been an NCO three years before, when I was a cadet. He and the other two platoon commanders of D Company were housed at the officers' quarters, away from the company, so we knew we wouldn't see him until after breakfast.

I noticed I wasn't the last one up. Bubbles and Joannic were still head down and eyes closed, despite the noise crackling from the radio, seemingly tuned just off the station so that the music and voices were distorted and annoying. It covered the sound of the groaning and the complaints of the young men as the dragged themselves out of bed, though.

I slipped carefully over the edge of my bunk so as not to step on Banzal, who was in the bunk below mine. He was sitting on the edge of his bed, lacing up his boots. He watched me warily over his glasses as I began to slide down. He kept his eye on me until I hit the floor.

I pulled on my pants and a T-shirt and headed for the washroom, which was through the door and across the hall. I opened the door and met Aleth Bruce, who was just making his way back from the shower, the slap-slap of his flip-flops announcing his approach in the almost pitch-black hallway. He breezed in with a towel over his shoulder, a bottle of shampoo in his hand, and what seemed to be an asphyxiating cloud of baby powder. It was a welcome change from the scent of the fourteen bodies in our quarters.

Aleth Bruce and I couldn't have been more physically different. He was taller than me, barrel-chested and powerful looking, whereas I was as thin as a rail. Anyone would have expected a stern look and a booming voice from him, but he wore only a perpetual smile and had the voice of a child. And he was a study in personal hygiene products: I had never seen so many small containers of creams, shampoos, and talcum powders in one place before.

I looked into the 10 Platoon barrack on my way to the washroom. This was a low, temporary-looking, one-storey building about twenty metres long. It contained forty-eight beds stacked in twos, lined up in two rows with an aisle down the middle. The cadets slept with their heads to the wall and their feet to the aisle. Looking in the doorway made it easy to see all the way down the line. The lights were still off in there and all was quiet.

From the air, each company looked like four long buildings joined to form a big cross. There was an orderly room (OR) building, with offices for the company CO and adjutant at one end and, in the middle, an administrative office—a large open area with a few desks, filing cabinets, and a bed for the duty officer to sleep on at night. A narrow hallway ran down the side of the building from the CO's office, past the adjutant's office and the admin area to where the four buildings met. The admin area was separated from the hallway by a counter and a low, swinging gate. The NCOs' quarters were at the other end of the OR building, where all the buildings joined together. The other three buildings in the complex housed the platoons, and came together at the washroom and a common area.

I crossed back through the common area from the washroom toward our quarters. In the darkness, the outline of freshly pressed uniforms was barely discernible. These were taken care of in the evenings, the irons going all the time in a competitive quest for the sharpest and longest-lasting pant-leg crease. Techniques differed about the best way to accomplish the perfect crease. Some preferred steam pressing. Most pressed their pants with a damp cloth over the pant leg; those who didn't usually ended up with ridiculous-looking dark and shiny inseams. I saw the most curious innovation, although I never used it, when a cadet turned his pants inside out and ran a bar of soap down the inside of the front and back creases. He then flipped the pants right-side out and ironed them with a wet cloth over the top. When he had finished he left them to cool for a few minutes before hanging them up for the night. He insisted that the soap held the creases longer and sharper than anything else.

During the evening routine, one half of the platoon would press and iron while the rest polished boots and brass. The boots were usually the last job of the day. Polishing boots is not something that can be hurried—one must gather the equipment: a can of shoe polish (never liquid polish), a brush to remove the dust, a cloth, an old toothbrush for the welts, and a cup of cold water (purists, of course, use spit, but water works just as well). The boys would sit on their own or in a group, talking quietly or hotly debating issues. Either way, the slow, rhythmic, and methodical hand movements and tiny circles delicately traced out with an index finger gently coaxed the shine from within the boots. When finished, the gleaming, mirror-like boots would be covered with a light cloth to keep the dust off and placed under the bunk to keep them safe from being tripped over in the night. No amount of apology would excuse a scuffed boot on inspection day. Well-shined boots were a source of pride for those with the knack, and a source of admiration or jealousy from those who couldn't quite get it.

On my way back into our quarters, I could see out the window the silhouette of the trees begin to appear. The sky was beginning to lighten, but then, "Oh hell, it's raining." A few other heads looked toward the window and groaned as the rain ran gently down the pane. I swung my bush jacket on, sat down on the edge of Banzal's bunk, and slipped on my boots. Any amount of rain meant we'd have to have the inspection inside, and an inside inspection added complications. There was a company inspection every morning, of course, but an inspection by the camp commander necessitated extra care. The results of this inspection would directly reflect our job performance, that of our company officers, and, of course, the company as a whole, so no amount of effort would be spared to make the company as organized and as clean as possible.

Every day, every bed had to be completely stripped, and the bedding folded and placed on the beds in the approved and identical way. On weekends, we could make the beds hospital-style, the way most beds are at home—except, of course, every one of our beds had to be made in the prescribed manner and look exactly alike. During the week, however, the beds had to be done evacuation-style, as if we were leaving and not coming back. Actually, it was a modified version of evacuation-style, as we left the mattresses flat; true evacuation-style would have seen the thin mattresses rolled up as well.

This morning, the bedding was removed, folded, and placed: blanket, sheet, blanket, sheet, pillowcase, and pillow on the top. All the folds of the bedding were lined up exactly and placed identically on each bed. It wasn't enough to have them neatly folded, either. The bedding had to be placed at the head of the bed and presented with no wrinkles, bends, dimples, dents, or creases. The stack had to be perfectly flat with the primary folds facing the foot of the bed and the secondary folds facing the entrance at the head of the platoon, and to look as though they were solid and fresh.

The process took every new cadet quite a while to master. As a cadet, I remember working at my bedding every morning for almost a week with unsatisfactory results, although it always looked reasonably good to me. I remember asking my section leader, Corporal Linton, if it was good enough.

"There is no such thing as good enough," he snapped. "It is either right or it is not done."

I did eventually master it, and I felt sure Linton would be pleased to hear that I snapped the same thing at my cadets each year. Of course, it was not about the bedding but about getting a task right. That seemed to be one of the objectives of all the training: if it wasn't right, it wasn't done.

Once the bedding was done, the bunks themselves had to be lined up perfectly. A cadet would be stationed at each end of the barrack to position the first and last bunks correctly. Then a squad of others would push, pull, nudge, and cajole the other bunks into line, while the folks at the ends acted like surveyors, waving their arms and calling out directions. The difference might be a matter of centimetres, but one of the surveyors would run to the bunk in question and nudge it, tap it, and kick it gently into place. Cadets were known to tie a string to the bunks at the ends and move the bunks in the middle up to the string until both legs were just touching it.

The windows, too, if they were open, had to be opened exactly the same height. We cut sticks all the same length to accomplish this because the wooden sash windows in the barracks were unreliable—they had a tendency to slip down when the weather changed. We would jam the sticks under the windows to hold them up, but place them inside the sash on the left and pull them forward so they couldn't be seen.

The last job before our morning inspection was the floor, which had to be swept and mopped—hence the rainy-day complication. To get the floor perfectly clean, someone had to stay behind to finish it off after the last person had left. But the whole base was built on sand, so when everyone returned after breakfast, they had to be certain not to track in sand on their boots. They couldn't knock the sand off their boots too hard outside for fear of scuffing those perfect shines, so someone had to stand at the door with a broom and sweep off the boot bottoms before they touched the floor. It took some time to get it right, which frustrated the folks outside who were getting their perfectly pressed pants and shined boots wetter and wetter as they waited in the rain. I didn't think about it at the time, but I should have looked for Mr. Soap-Creases. I can't imagine what happened to those soapy pants in the rain.

Once everyone was standing at the foot of their bunk waiting for the inspecting officer to arrive, the sweepers began their last pass through the barrack, straining their eyes to see any sand on the floor and scoop it up. Sometimes a few grains would escape the usually eagle-eyed sweepers. If they were under a bunk or in a corner, they would be of little consequence, but down the centre line of the barrack was a different story. The crunch of a few tiny grains of sand under the boot of the colonel or regimental sergeant major during the silence of the inspection would be damning. The near miraculous thing was that a perfect barrack was always achieved, and always achieved before 0730.

I had another look out the window while I laced up my boots. The sky was lighter, but it was raining harder now. I pulled my pant-leg cuffs up to my thighs and just above the knees clipped on my weights—a snake of two-centimetre lead pieces sewn into cotton tubes about a centimetre around and thirty centimetres long; the ends snapped together and formed a loose ring around the leg, holding the pants taut and giving the pant legs a perfectly straight line and removing any fold or break. I pulled my right pant leg over the weights and down to my ankle again. I grabbed hold of the cuff by the inseam and outer seam and lined up the hem with the second lace hole of my boot. I held onto the seams and pulled straight out at the sides, which brought the crease flush with the front of my ankle at the centre of my boot. With my thumbs as a guide, I folded the seams forward toward the front of my leg, keeping the crease in the dead centre, and held on with one hand while I got ready to wrap my puttees around my ankle to bind my pants to my boots.

Puttees look like cloth bandages, about seventy-five centimetres long and eight centimetres wide. At one end, they taper to a point and then continue into a forty-five-centimetre narrow cotton ribbon. Enlisted personnel wore olive-coloured puttees; officers' puttees were khaki-coloured. I wrapped one olive puttee on my right ankle, then I did the left side. Some people would pull the seams of their pants to the rear of the leg, but I found that rolling to the rear put too much stress on the front of the pant leg and flattened out the crease faster. Like everyone else, I wanted my creases to last the full day, so I rolled them forward. Everyone had his peculiar little secret tricks—that was one of mine.

With both puttees wrapped tightly around my ankles, I stood up to let the weights drop inside my pants from above my knees to the bottom of my bound pant leg. I snapped on my web belt and told Bruce and Medvescek that I would see them in the platoon. Medvescek had a knack for getting there first, so it was a small victory for me to be able to get to the barrack before him today. I smiled to myself in quiet triumph. I slipped on my beret, left our little room, and walked past the shower room door and into the 10 Platoon cadet barrack. I checked my watch—it was 0559. A few heads rose up like prairie dogs to look at me as I stepped into the room, but the majority of the heads were still on their pillows.

"Everybody, up!" I said, as I started walking slowly through the barrack. I didn't shout, but I was loud enough to be heard easily. "Come on, out of bed. Don't be lazy! Wade, get up you slacker. You, too, Botosan! Vallée! Get a move on!"

Every morning I said the same things, as my sergeant had done when I was a cadet. These words were a tradition. Only the names changed. The cadets always needed a little encouragement to get them going, just as I had as a cadet.

In a matter of minutes the platoon looked as busy as an anthill, with people rolling out of bed, moving to the showers and back, dressing, sweeping, folding bedding, and getting the barrack ready for inspection. Clean wasn't enough, though. The cadets knew by now there was an official method to perform every task and a prescribed way to present every result.

By this time, my corporals had joined me, and together we directed the activity. Medvescek got the sweepers started, while Bruce and Souva supervised the bunk alignment and the exterior cleaning. There wasn't much cleaning to do outside—just the occasional scrap of paper or cigarette butt that had blown over from somewhere else. A cigarette butt wouldn't have come from anyone in our company. Whether they smoked or not, cadets were soon taught to field strip cigarettes—tearing the remains into such tiny pieces as to be undetectable on the ground, even to the point of shredding the filters into strands that might look like bits of dandelion fluff.

While the barrack cleaning was under way, I headed back to the

NCOs' quarters to get my own bedding in order and to do my part in cleaning up our area. Bruce and Medvescek had already finished their bedding. Souva had started his and would finish after the cadets left for breakfast. It was like a tag team. I hurried through my own housekeeping duties and scurried back to the platoon to find that the barrack was close to inspection ready.

Breakfast Parade

As I entered the barrack that Tuesday morning, Bob Gibeault poked his head into the room and boomed, "Breakfast parade!" In less than ten seconds, the barrack was empty and so quiet that I could hear myself breathe. It was Bob's day to get the company to their meals, so I walked down the centre of the empty barrack, looking it over and making notes of what had to be finished before the inspection.

Each day, the sergeants and corporals took turns with the meal parade responsibilities. Outside, the company was formed up on the company parade square, dressed, turned, and marched toward the mess. My footsteps thundered on the wooden floor in the empty room as I made my way through the barrack, checking. There wasn't much left to do. The cadets had learned a lot in three weeks, and had prepared for the inspection with a minimum of supervision, acting like a well-organized team.

In the distance I could hear the company being marched away to the mess for breakfast, while the NCOs called the cadence, alternating in both French and English. The base was mostly francophone, and almost everything, from the general course instruction and words of command to extracurricular activities like the sports we played and the movies we screened, was conducted in French. In fact, out of the twelve or more companies, ours was considered the only English-speaking one, and even then only one of the three platoons—mine—was entirely anglophone; one was bilingual and the other was francophone.

For all the stories over the years of hostility and animosity between the French and English in Quebec, I never witnessed much friction beyond playful competitiveness on the base. There was none of that in our company, and we had some francophones who spoke no English and some anglophones who spoke not a word of French. In my experience, most everyone got along, and many took the time to learn at least a bit of the others' language, usually beginning with the most colourful obscenities. Once in a while, at the beginning, we would let one of the cadets call the cadence while we were marching. We had to put a stop to it, though. The anglophones enjoyed calling the cadence in French and the francophones would call it in English, except they would call out their own versions. The French would chant, "Left…left…lêve ta patte, puis pisse dans l'poche." And the English would answer with, "Gauche…gauche…go shit in the corner." It was all in fun, but we couldn't let it continue.

There were forty-seven cadets in my platoon. Although they had been here for three weeks, I was still getting to know them. Some were easy to know because of their large personalities or because they were troublemakers or just always seemed to be around me. Others, though, were quieter and kept to themselves. My brother, Nick, was a cadet in 10 Platoon. Karl Medvescek's brother Ingo was a cadet as well. Karl and I had an agreement that, if the need arose, we would handle each other's sibling issues; that way, we hoped to avoid complaints of nepotism or sibling rivalry. So far, however, there had been no issues—both were exemplary cadets. Nick and I occasionally would exchange a few words when no one was around or acknowledge each other in the distance, but otherwise I had little contact with him. That was the way he wanted it.

Paul Wheeler breezed in to my platoon barrack while I finished taking notes. Paul was a great friend and full of fun. We had come from the same home unit and often hung around together. We had trained together for a few years and risen through the ranks at our home unit before coming to Valcartier as NCOs.

Paul had a gift for keeping a deadly serious face while engaged in mischief. He also had a knack for cartoon-like voices and could

Members of 10 Platoon take a break on an armoured personnel
carrier a few days before the explosion.

utter them quietly enough to be barely audible. But I always seemed to be within earshot, and the combination of Paul's squeaky voices and having to stand at attention on parade made me an irresistible target for him. No one in authority ever suspected him, though. Whenever a question arose of who was responsible for some devilry, he would push his aviator-style glasses further up his nose and look around, as if he, too, was looking for the culprit. Inevitably, they would all turn toward me as I shook, struggling to contain my laughter. Paul was smart and he made us all laugh, but he took everything he worked at seriously. He treated the cadets respectfully and they respected him in return.

"You coming to breakfast, Gerry?"

"Yeah, let's go."

He tossed me my trench coat and we left for the mess.

The wet air was still scented with the remnants of the mosquito fogging truck that had passed through the camp the evening before. The fogging truck would weave its way periodically through the camp, announcing its approach with an obnoxious and grating hum, while trailing a thick, bluish fog behind it. If the day was windless, some of the heavy fog would waft upward into the trees, but the bulk of it would drift horizontally into the undergrowth and the bush along the roadway. It would hang in the air and in the bush for a few minutes before slowly sinking to the ground. For a short time after the truck had gone, the area would have a dreamlike, fantasy atmosphere for those who could ignore the grating sound of the departing truck and the oily, sinister smell of the haze.

Paul and I took a shortcut between the other companies, through the trees, by the camp admin building, and around the quartermaster building. The company was marching along the road that ran around the perimeter of the camp. Taking the shortcut with Paul was always an adventure.

Among the officers in the camp were a few unilingual francophones, two of whom, second lieutenants, Paul had it in for in particular. These unsuspecting and naive fellows had the misfortune to wear pants that didn't quite fit, marking them as targets for Paul's humour. Their pants were a bit tight, but what made them look ridiculous was that they were about five centimetres too short. In the 1970s, if pant hems were well above the ground, we referred to them as flood pants.

We met these second lieutenants almost every day. Second lieutenants technically were officers, but only one step above an officer cadet and treated as glorified trainees. Consequently, the respect they were generally given was superficial. Paul had begun greeting them every morning by quickly saying, "When's the flood, Sir," in the same way he would have said, "Good morning, Sir." That kind of disrespect would have been enough to have us severely reprimanded, but we felt like we were living on the edge. He would say it with a deadly serious face as we gave them our best salutes on the way by—indeed, our salutes were so crisp they bordered on violent. The lieutenants must have been only recently promoted, because looking at their faces as they returned the salutes, we could see they were not only flattered but also felt very important. One morning, though, the whole game almost backfired on us. We were on our way to the mess when we sighted the innocent second lieutenants in the distance, rounding the corner of the quartermaster building. Paul muttered to me, "Ahoy, Noah!" As we were about to pass them, our hands shot up to salute. This time, one of the officers pre-empted our salutation by slurring a cordial "Za flud," on his way by. He evidently thought it was a legitimate English greeting. We were shocked into silence, breaking it only to vow to avoid these officers for the rest of the summer.

Paul and I arrived at the mess just as the last few files of cadets were sent in. We followed behind them with Bob Gibeault, picking up our trays and joining the food line. There was no use trying to speak to one another in the deafening sounds of the mess hall: pots and lids banging together, exhaust fans humming, plates clanging as they are filled with food, utensils crashing in the bins and then clicking on plates, leftovers being scraped into garbage cans. Occasionally a plate or stack of plates would hit the concrete floor with a crash, inevitably followed by a cheer as the clumsy oaf either slunk away or brazened out the acclaim. Shouts or outbursts were strictly forbidden, but there were also hundreds of voices competing to be heard. Each small noise contributed to an incessant roar that grew as the crowd expanded and slowly abated as the mess emptied between the meal services.

I had just made it to the front of the line when I saw Nick leaving the mess through the back door with a few other cadets who had finished eating. I caught his eye and he smiled back at me as he stepped through the exit door. Being the last group into the mess had its drawbacks. By the time they have served twenty-five hundred or so meals, the cooks are in a bit of a hurry to get the meal over with, and they rush through the last hundred or so. Sometimes things at the end of the line can be a bit overcooked, or worse, undercooked. We were the last ones in that morning and consequently had to suffer the latecomers' breakfast penance. It was a relief that morning to leave the mess for the quiet walk back to the company.

Inspection

After a breakfast of half-cooked eggs, slippery bacon, and muddy coffee, Paul and I headed back to our platoons. Getting to 10 Platoon, I could see through the open door that the cadets were just finishing up the cleaning. Paul continued on around the outside of the orderly room toward 12 Platoon.

The thumping of my boots on the steps alerted the cadet with the broom, who had his back to me. He was at the door in no time to brush the sand off my boots. As he swept, I watched two cadets, Jimmy Howell and Robin Hughes, moving from bunk to bunk making sure that every one of the combination locks on the barrack boxes was pointing up at zero. They had done a great job—the place looked spotless.

To give them a minute or two more to get organized, I went to my quarters to drop off my trench coat and then returned. I walked to the head of the room to check the alignment down the row of bunks on the right. Aleth Bruce scrutinized the row on the other side. A few of the cadets watched me as I lingered over the alignment with one eye closed for effect. One made frantic hand signals to the other end of the room to shoo people out of my line of vision. I craned my neck a few times and affected a quizzical look accompanied by a mumbled "Mmmmmf?" to create a little doubt in their minds.

"Good," I said suddenly. "Corporal Bruce?"

"Good on this side, Sergeant," he said with formality.

"Thank you, Corporal Bruce."

They all looked pleased and yet a bit anxious as they milled around, waiting for the inspection to be called. They all stood, of course. No one dared to sit on a bed that had been perfectly sculpted and aligned for the occasion, and sitting down on anything meant jeopardizing a perfectly pressed uniform.

I made my way to the orderly room to see if I could get a decent cup of coffee while waiting for the colonel's arrival. Fullum, the company clerk, made great coffee and always had a pot going. When I reached the OR, however, I found the pot empty, clean, and cold. Disappointed, I returned to the NCOs' quarters, where Karl Medvescek was hanging up his trench coat. He gave me a look, rolled his eyes, and pointed at Fullum's bunk, which was still occupied.

Bubbles Fullum: I don't know why he was called Bubbles. He was slim, didn't wear glasses, and didn't chew gum. As far as I knew, he had simply arrived with that nickname. Fullum usually took his time getting up, because his duties weren't the same as ours. Clerical duties meant he typically didn't have to get the cadets to the mess early in the morning, although he frequently did because I think he enjoyed it. He was easygoing, and his facility in both French and English amazed me. He could switch between languages on the fly, even in mid-sentence. He was given some leeway about sleeping in a bit and missing breakfast because typing up reports and organizing company schedules and activities meant his workdays sometimes went beyond ours. This morning, though, he had to be up—the inspection would include our quarters as well.

Medvescek and I looked at each another and nodded. Gently, we peeled the covers off Fullum to expose him to the cold, damp Valcartier morning. He opened one eye, groaned, and pulled himself out of bed. We left him to get ready.

At 0730, the cadets were formed up in front of their bunks, standing easy, and awaiting the colonel's inspection. The rain was coming down harder now, larger drops tapping on the roof like a drum roll as the time slowly passed. Bruce and Medvescek stood at the head of the barrack and ensured the alignment of the cadets in front of the bunks. The cadets at either end were placed at the right distance from their beds and the others in between were shuffled forward or backward until the toes of their boots, like their bunks, were all lined up. Then, we waited.

At about 0805, the rain intensified. Through the barrack windows, I saw a jeep drive up inside the company lines. Out of the jeep jumped Colonel Whitelaw and Regimental Sergeant Major (RSM) Clérmont Morin, who hurried through the rain into the company through the OR entrance. I quietly called out, "10 Platoon!" Heads snapped forward and hands shot behind, and the cadets stood silently at ease, waiting to be called to attention.

The colonel was met at the OR door by our company commander, Major Robert Brochu, and company sergeant major, Sergeant Charles Gutta. Moments later, we heard their heavy footsteps on the wooden floor in the hallway coming toward our barrack. As the colonel stuck his foot inside the barrack, I called the platoon to attention. Fifty-one pairs of feet pounded to attention in unison, making the wooden floor shake. I snapped my hand up to salute. The colonel glanced at me, his face serious, returned the salute, and then moved on with Major Brochu and RSM Morin trailing behind.

Our RSM had a stern look that would freeze my insides. His eyes would seem to burn into me, and I never saw him smile. Whenever he spoke, I always felt it was going to be unpleasant for me. Once, when I was walking alone back to the company after a meal, I heard him in the distance behind me yell, "You!" His shouting voice was unmistakable as it echoed off the buildings. I swung around on the spot to face him and stood at attention, wondering what I had done to provoke his ire. I was holding my breath, preparing for the worst. He was about fifty metres away. I noticed that there were twenty-five or thirty of us scattered around, but now everyone was at attention, facing him in a wide, sprinkled semicircle.

Then I realized the RSM's gaze was fixed in the direction of some poor sod who'd had his hands in his pockets. The sod was smiling, looking around for the unlucky recipient of this most unwanted attention. Then, as if a light bulb had switched on over his head, it dawned on him that he was the focus, and his expression changed to shocked horror. Whether he realized on his own or someone near him whispered what was up, he drew his hands out of his pockets so quickly that they ended up in the air as if he were under arrest. The RSM stayed where he was and waited until the fellow snapped to attention before turning away and heading in the other direction. I started breathing again, but not one of us moved until the RSM was around the corner and out of sight.

As Colonel Whitelaw moved past me and into my platoon to begin the inspection, the RSM stopped to glare at me. He stood at a distance that we would now say was well within my personal space—he was so close that it would have been difficult for me to focus my eyes on him. Then he took a step back to look me over quickly, while I stood at attention, breathing only enough to stay alive. He then turned to Bruce, Souva, and Medvescek before moving on, never compromising his ramrod posture as he walked. Out of the corner of my eye, I saw him carefully lay his drill cane on the table just opposite me. I couldn't move my eyes. He would have picked that up. In fact, I was sure he would be looking for that; I certainly would have been.

Standing at attention is an exercise in self-control and self-discipline, as well as a gesture of respect. Standing perfectly straight and perfectly still in front of a superior shows not only submission but also an acknowledgement of trust. It is almost canine, in the way a dog will present its neck or belly to a more dominant dog, secure in the knowledge that the higher-ranking dog will not take advantage of the submissive dog. There is an understanding that a superior is responsible for your general welfare, just as my cadets knew they were my responsibility.

When the RSM followed the colonel into the platoon, he left behind his drill cane—usually clamped tightly under his left arm—on the table, presumably needing both hands to take notes during the inspection. That gave us a rare chance to examine the cane at close range, although no one dared to touch it.

It was an interesting drill cane. Technically, it was a pace stick, consisting of two pieces of wood, tapered and shod, with steel tips at the bottom. It was ninety-one centimetres long, hinged at the top, and able to unfold like a drafting compass. It could be opened to fixed distances to measure things precisely: thirty-inch quick-march paces, forty-inch double-time paces, the twelve-inch distance between your heels when standing at ease, among other things. A pace stick's utility, however, is secondary. Its primary function is to identify the rank of RSM, the highest ranking enlisted personnel. The RSM is responsible for standards and discipline in the battalion. His word is law, and there is only ever one RSM per battalion.

The colonel slowed his pace once inside the platoon and moved down the centre line, casting his eyes over the room and the cadets, who were standing at attention with their eyes fixed straight ahead. The RSM, on the other hand, applied a more critical eye, looking under the bunks, the space between the wall and the bunks, and inside the window casements. I wasn't worried. The whole platoon had worked diligently to prepare for this; everything was just right. The RSM made notes anyway. He even looked up toward the ceiling. I don't know what he hoped to see up there. I noticed that, as he passed the cadets, a few had followed him with their eyes for a fleeting moment. They had been clever enough to wait until he had passed, so he wouldn't notice their slight movement. I noticed it, though.

When the colonel was finished with our platoon, he and the RSM moved briskly out toward the next platoon. I loudly called my platoon to stand at ease, to let the other platoon sergeants know the inspection party was on its way to them. It was a signal we had established in advance so the next platoon wouldn't be caught unaware. I then told my platoon to stand easy, which meant they could move their heads and arms but their feet had to stay planted and, of course, there was no talking.

The RSM's cane was still on the table, so the corporals and I silently joked about stealing and hiding it. Using mostly eye movements and hand gestures, we illustrated where we would hide it on our person and how we would feign ignorance of its whereabouts when questioned.

We explored everything from hiding it down a pant-leg or down the back of a jacket to miming hiding it like a sword-swallower. The cadets quite enjoyed this bit of irreverence from their NCOs, but not a word was spoken or a chuckle heard.

From the other end of the company complex, I heard Bob Gibeault loudly call his platoon to stand at ease. The platoon inspections were finished. Without much delay, the RSM fairly burst back into our platoon to retrieve his pace stick. He scrutinized us standing as he had left us before slowly moving his severe gaze to the pace stick. It was almost as if he had expected us to have handled it and was disappointed that he hadn't caught us at it. He scooped it up and was gone.

We listened to the inspection party move from the NCO quarters to the OR, where I could hear Major Brochu offer the colonel some coffee. What coffee? I thought we were out. They couldn't have had any, as they immediately left the company and drove off. With the colonel and RSM gone, we received word from Sergeant Gutta to start the cadets' training.

Drill

Sergeant Charles Gutta, our company sergeant major (CSM) and my immediate superior, was in charge of the NCOs, company discipline, and certain aspects of training. He was a regular career soldier and a sergeant with the 12th Armoured Regiment (le 12ᵉ Régiment blindé du Canada), which was stationed permanently at Valcartier.

Sergeant Gutta was a serious man. I don't think I ever saw him smile. He moved his compact, solid frame with purpose and economy. Although he was a man of few words, whenever he spoke to any of us, it was understood both by him and by us that we would get the job done. There were never any questions, and he never repeated himself. He not only understood his own job and performed it to the letter, but also he understood the jobs of those around him. Whether they were cadets, NCOs, or officers, Sergeant Gutta seemed to make it his task to ensure they understood their jobs. We looked up to him and the officers deferred to him. We, the NCOs, knew we could count on him for anything.

"Right or wrong, I will back you up one hundred per cent, no matter what," he had said when we were first assigned to D Company. "But when I do," he continued with a pointed stare, "you had better be right."

We knew he would do anything for us, but he had a price. He wanted nothing short of one hundred per cent from us and we tried to give him just that. He seemed to have connections almost everywhere; he knew how to obtain things and how to get things done. Once, before the cadets had arrived, we were scheduled to have an inspection. He thought everyone's hair looked a bit shaggy, so he said he would arrange for a barber to come in. When Corporal Banzal suggested we just go to the camp barber, Gutta swung around and his deep blue eyes bored into the corporal, stopping him in his tracks, "No, that man is a butcher. I'll arrange a barber," he growled. Then he quietly added, "Someone owes me a favour," and he walked into the next office.

The inspection earlier in the morning mustn't have gone too badly because Sergeant Gutta said nothing about it. If there had been some glaring errors or deficiencies, he would have let us know right away. Instead, he told us to get the day's training under way. This morning it would be drill. We were about three weeks away from the final inspection, when the whole battalion would be on parade for the graduation exercises. The marching, turning, and wheeling instruction we would give the cadets today during drill would be the foundation of their preparation for that final parade.

It wasn't always drill, although wherever we went, we would march there. All kinds of courses and lectures were held for the cadets, as part of the Cadet Leader Program, to train and prepare them to return to their units as the next generation of leaders. Besides drill, there was orienteering, bush craft, swimming, canoeing, survival, bridge building, athletics, small arms safety, shooting, driver safety, first aid, and cultural activities such as trips to Quebec City to see the historical sites and explore the Plains of Abraham.

Upon being given the order to form up outside, the cadets quickly hustled out into the rain, but were then told to go back inside for their rain ponchos, which none of them had thought to don. Part of learning to be a leader is also learning to be a responsible follower. They had done the right thing by reacting to the order immediately. Anyone who has tried to organize a group of teenage boys to move quickly and without complaint knows that this is a near miracle. I should have been clearer, though, and mentioned the ponchos earlier. The brownish green poncho was like a large square rubberized canvas sheet with grommets and snaps all around the edges and a drawstring hood in the centre. It was a marvel of multiple uses, with a bit of creativity. Two of them could be snapped together and slung over a pole or branch to make an improvised shelter for two. It could serve as a hammock, stretcher, or travois, or catch rainwater for drinking. When I was training in the Rocky Mountains, I had even seen it used to make a sort of canoe: the poncho was stretched over a frame made of saplings and green twigs so that the snaps and grommets were above the water line. The hood, which fell below the waterline, was tightly tied off with the drawstring to keep the water out. As rain gear, however, the poncho was only passable. It fell to just below our knees, so that, in a heavy rain, all the water that hit the upper body was just rerouted to our legs, soaking our pants below the knees, rendering a two-tone look, and, of course, drenching our leather boots. In hot weather, if we had to wear the heavy poncho for any length of time, the humidity would make us as damp as if we weren't wearing one at all.

The cadets unrolled their ponchos, climbed under them, then bustled, rustling and swishing, out of the barrack and into the rain. Reforming ranks, they marched off to training. Walking in step with their arms restricted at their sides by the drab-coloured rain gear, they looked like a group of monks in procession. We headed to the base parade square, which was quite a distance away, up the hill from the cadet camp on the base's main road. We had to climb a long, wide flight of wooden stairs to reach the parade square, so the cadets had to break step—a hundred and twenty people walking in step could stress and snap a structure like that. Even out of step, we sometimes could feel the wooden stairs bending and bouncing.

It was a dreary march in the rain. My trench coat and beret were getting heavier with the falling water as we marched to the ponchos' swishing cadence. Thus cloaked, the cadets would not be hearing much more than the rustling accompanied by the pock-pock-pock of heavy raindrops on their hoods. I remembered walking under a poncho when I was a cadet. The noise of the rain on the hood all but drowned out the sounds around us, as we walked with nothing in our field of vision except the back of the hooded head in front. Because the hoods restricted our peripheral vision, we would have to turn our whole body to look at something while walking. Inevitably, this disorienting movement would cause someone to trip and fall, the whole group behind tumbling in turn like a multiple-car pileup on an icy road. We always tried to explain this phenomenon to the cadets the first time they donned ponchos, but they would look at us as though we were crazy. But every year someone would oblige and prove the point. Not today, though; today, everyone stayed on their feet.

Reaching the parade square, we saw it was covered in shallow puddles. To drill on a water covered surface is not practical, so Sergeant Gutta instructed us to bring the group to building #502, an adjacent hangar-sized structure used for the maintenance of artillery pieces. Its ceiling was very high, and a huge bank of windows all around the top provided more than adequate light to train. There was plenty of room in there for us: with its empty, flat, and shiny concrete floor, building #502 looks as though it had been designed as an indoor parade square.

As soon as we were inside, the cadets peeled off their ponchos, hung them on hooks that lined the walls, and were quickly formed up again as a company. There they stood in three ranks at attention, their rain-soaked pants dark green from the knees down, as were their cap visors, which had poked out of their poncho hoods.

We divided the company into platoons, and marched them off to separate corners of the building, where they were split into squads or sections. Each corporal drilled a section of ten to fifteen cadets in the basics and practised them for about thirty minutes. Once the sections were working as one, they were reformed into their platoons. Then the platoons practised for a while before they were brought together to form the whole company.

The noise was unbelievable. Loud commands echoed in the cavernous building, feet slammed to the ground. Left turn! Swish, bang! About turn! Swi-ish bang! And they were all together—well, mostly: three corporals in each of three platoons meant nine sets of commands competing to be heard. I walked from section to section of my platoon, making small adjustments to the cadets' foot positions or keeping them in step as they marched.

I came upon Medvescek as he was working with his section, and walked behind them as he gave commands from the front. He was very particular about how he wanted the section to perform these drill movements. His own movements were precise and exact. On parade, he was as straight as an arrow and as sharp as a tack. He wanted no less from his section. He would call out a command, and if the response was not what he expected, he would yell, "As you were!" That meant disregard the last thing that happened; go back to what you were doing before and we'll try it again. For instance, if a senior officer entered and a room was called to attention, the officer might say, "As you were," to let everyone know the visit was a casual one and that they could relax—as much as to say, "Pretend I am not here; pretend it never happened."

Medvescek called his platoon to attention. Most of them did so together. "As you were," he said, sourly.

The morning passed striving to achieve basic drill movements executed in time, while the cadets' pants slowly dried to one colour. Drill was an important aspect of our training, however, because it bred discipline and taught the group to act together as a unit. There was something satisfying, too, about the sound of our forty, fifty, or one hundred pairs of boots coming to attention or marching in unison with arms swinging shoulder high. I felt proud to be part of a tight, focused, and impressive unit. This sense of pride and feeling of unity are most important to hold a platoon together as a team.

Then I discovered my team was being pulled apart from the inside.

Goon Squad

My platoon had a problem: a "goon squad" was working on the smaller and less confident cadets. It wasn't hardcore bullying, just adolescent male pecking-order posturing. Nonetheless, I wasn't terribly happy about the situation. As a young cadet and as a boy growing up, I had been on the receiving end of bullying, so I was particularly angry that this was going on at all. As well, it flew in the face of the leadership training for which the cadets were at the camp in the first place.

To foster a sense of democratic leadership, we had spoken to all the cadets soon after their arrival and suggested they pick someone who would speak for the platoon if there was some general problem—a shortage of hot water, something broken, light bulbs out, a shortage of toilet tissue, or something of that nature. These might be things neither I nor the other NCOs would be aware of, and having a spokesman would save us from hearing about the same problem from ten different people—or worse, not hearing about it at all.

Unfortunately, the spokesman the platoon chose had decided to appropriate his responsibility for power. In truth, I didn't think it was entirely his fault; I felt he was being led astray by some of his peers. A small group seemed to have been commandeered by a cadet named Eddy Vallée. He was larger than most of the others and more aggressive. In front of me, he was a loutish joker; out of my sight, I learned he was intimidating some of the others. It seemed possible that he was also intimidating the spokesman, who tried to diminish the risk of Vallée's turning on him by going along with Vallée and his cronies.

Thus was formed my platoon's bully boys, who were coercing some of the others into working faster or harder or pestering them for not measuring up to some unspoken rules. The recipient of at least one act of aggression was one of the quieter cadets, Sven Engles. He came to me on the quiet to report that Vallée had roughed him up and he wanted it to stop, but he didn't want the bullies to know he had said anything to me. On this day of drill practice, we had just found out about these bullies, and we were looking for a solution to the problem. We had talked among ourselves and had spoken to Vallée to let him know he was being watched. We were determined to find a solution ourselves rather than bring it up the chain of command to Sergeant Gutta.

I glanced at my watch: 1119. Time to head back and get ready for lunch. My stomach rumbled to confirm. I decided to let Bob Gibeault know it was probably time to get the cadets back. After a series of hand signals across the huge room indicating the time, the platoon sergeants had their platoons ready to move out. The rain had stopped, so the cadets collected their ponchos from the hooks and rolled them up to carry under their left arms. Gibeault gave the command to start marching back.

I decided to trail behind with Bruce, who was having a problem with a certain troublemaker, Ron Botosan. Botosan felt he had to let everyone know how much smarter he was than anyone else. We suspected he was involved with the platoon bullies because he was often in the company of Vallée and was always quick to laugh at Vallée's smart-aleck remarks, egging him on to push the envelope. So we had begun to watch Botosan closely as well. Our platoon was at the end of the company column today, and Botosan was in the last file. I couldn't hear exactly what was going on, but I could see, even at a distance, that Botosan's jaws were working overtime. He talked incessantly; moreover, he was disrespectful.—with him it was not just that there was an occasional difference of opinion, but that he was obstinate and abusive.

I slung my trench coat over my left arm, and hustled to catch up to the company, which was already at the quick-march. Just as I reached the rear of the platoon, I heard Bruce say to Botosan, "Now, just keep your mouth shut!"; then, in long strides, he moved swiftly to the front of the platoon. I knew Bruce was doing him a favour by walking away before Botosan could get himself into more trouble by trying to get the last word in. He was very disruptive, and we wanted him returned to his home unit before he could negatively influence the others, but we had to get him on an inexcusable infraction. Not that we wanted him to commit one; we simply hoped to catch him at what we suspected he was already doing.

Not wanting to interfere but still keeping an eye on Botosan, I remained silent and positioned myself just to the right and a half-pace behind him. We were crossing through a parking lot and approaching the top side of the long staircase when Botosan looked over at me and said, "Bruce is fucking stupid."

Besides the inexcusable statement, which I only thought I heard him make, he shouldn't have been talking in the ranks, and he shouldn't have turned his head from the front while marching. I couldn't believe my ears.

"What?" I said.

"Bruce is a stupid fucker," he sneered without a hint of apology.

Although he'd confirmed what I thought he had said, it was too insubordinate to believe fully. For a cadet to say something like that about an NCO to a senior NCO was unthinkable. I had trained and worked with Bruce for a few years, and I knew he was not only intelligent but also reasonable and sensitive. He was not one to fly off the handle. I needed Botosan to speak loud enough so there were more witnesses. So I said again, "What?!"

"Corporal Bruce is fucking stupid!" he shouted back at me. I saw the eyes of the cadets in the vicinity widen in disbelief as they continued to face front and march.

I had him.

"Keep your mouth closed, your eyes front, and swing your arms, Botosan!" I snapped.

Mentally, I was already preparing the report I would write. Attending the camp was a privilege reserved for those training for leadership positions. Anyone who ignored the chain of command or was unable to show respect to his superiors clearly was not ready for a leadership role or leadership training. I would make a verbal report to Sergeant Gutta when I got back to the company and then document the incident on paper. This was going to be Botosan's ticket home.

As soon as we arrived back at the company, Bob Gibeault dismissed the cadets. They had a bit of time to clean up and relax before lunch parade. I was on my way into the orderly room to write the report when I was stopped in my tracks.

"Sergeant! Sergeant Fostaty, they've done it again!" I didn't even have to see the boy to know who it was. I stopped on the stairs, sighed, and pivoted to face him.

"Who has done what, Mangos?" I started back down again.

Othon Mangos always seemed to have a crisis brewing. It was hard to take his crises very seriously, though, because he always had a smile on his face, even when he tried to affect a serious look. And he always had the sort of crisis that would make me roll my eyes. For instance, he and his buddy David Malcolm seemed to make it their objective to get out of some part of the training every day. There was never any big trouble. In fact, the two of them really grew on me. I was always interested to see what they would come up with next. They were quite a team to watch. It was almost like a choreographed dance. There was different music every day, but the dance steps were always the same. One would have a problem and be describing it in detail, while the other would stand beside him, wide-eyed and nodding frantically in earnest support. They would reverse roles almost every time. They were smaller than the other cadets, and at fourteen they were among the youngest in the platoon. With the recent news of bullying going on, I didn't mind taking the time to hear them out. Usually they would complain to me that something was missing from their kit—pants, a shirt, or a cap—and they were convinced it had been stolen.

They were always up to something. One day, after finishing a long lecture in a hot, airless marquee tent, I was heading back into the company to clean up. On my way up the three steps into the building, I thought I heard a rustling and some chatter under the barrack. I backed down the stairs and lowered myself to investigate. There was a crawl space of about forty-five centimetres under the barrack, and there were Mangos and Malcolm lying prone. When they saw me glaring at them, they each struck an expression I was sure they thought would convince me of their innocence. Their dust-covered faces broke into unnatural smiles as they stopped in mid-sentence. I couldn't imagine what they were doing under the barrack, but before I could even begin to ask, they spoke first.

"Good afternoon, Sergeant," began Mangos, as he propped himself up on his elbows, bumping his head on the underside of the building. "You see, we..."

"Never mind!" I barked back at them.

Mangos was now rubbing the top of his head. The look of them under the building trying to look nonchalant was comical, but there was no way I could let them know I was succumbing to the hilarity. As Mangos continued to rub his head where he had bumped it, I felt a smile beginning. I had to bite the inside of my cheek and stand up so that they couldn't see my face. They were still under the building.

"Go and get cleaned up. I want to see you later!" I growled.

I never did find out what they were up to under there. I didn't think I could pursue the matter with a straight face, so I avoided them for the rest of the day and just let it go. I am sure they thought they'd had the better of me, when it was really I who had escaped them.

There was no escaping them this time, however. I was trapped. Mangos was striding up to me, his face screwed up into his version of a frown. I wanted to get to the typewriter to start my report, but if I let him begin one of his long preambles, it would seriously cut into my already limited amount of time. I stopped him in his tracks with, "Now, what is the problem?"

"They're gone!" he said, with his hands stretched out wide, shaking his head. "They must know my combination."

Wait a minute, this wasn't right. Where was Malcolm? I looked from side to side and sure enough, Malcolm came around the corner, hand stretched out in front of him like an opera singer. "It's gone!"

They both began to rattle on and overlap each other's explanation. I held my hands out and snapped, "Wait! One at a time!"

Apparently, Mangos's pants were gone for the third time and Malcolm couldn't find his bush cap. This was nothing new. One day they would be missing something, and the next day they would be missing something else but wearing what they had been missing the previous day. I assured them we would find the missing articles after lunch and sent them on their way. Whether they were the victims of a series of pranks or they were misplacing the items, I knew that even without any intervention on my part, the lost items would turn up.

I looked at my watch: 1135, time for lunch parade. Great, I had missed starting the report before leaving for lunch. I would have to get to the mess, eat in a hurry, and get back here to get it done. I quickly went to each platoon and announced, "Parade de dîner! Lunch parade!" The barracks emptied and the cadets began to form up for the trip to the mess. I had a quick discussion with Sergeant Gutta about Botosan's behaviour while I watched the cadets form up outside the OR.

"Get a report written and get it to me right after lunch," he said without hesitation. "We'll take it up with Captain Boisvert then." Captain Clément Boisvert was our company adjutant. Our company commander, Major Brochu, was away for the afternoon, so Captain Boisvert would step in for this disciplinary matter.

Although it was Bob Gibeault's day to march the company to the mess, I went along, too. This morning's training was still fresh in their minds as they marched crisply, swinging their arms and then halting at the mess in perfect time. Their right turn in front of the mess was perfect, and the whole company slammed feet to attention as one. I was impressed and proud, and I could see that they were, too. I knew Gibeault was—his commands got a little louder and drawn out to give them a more formal air, so that other arriving companies could appreciate what hard work could accomplish. We sent the cadets into the mess file by file, three at a time. Once they were inside, the NCOs followed, lining up behind them. The cadets would finish lunch on their own time and leisurely make their own way back to the company. I ate speedily and hurried back to write the report.

Safety Lecture

"This afternoon we can relax," groaned Karl Medvescek with a smile and a stretch, as he read the afternoon syllabus hanging on the orderly room wall above the coffee machine.

He had just returned from Tuesday's lunch. The cadets were to have an explosives safety lecture in the afternoon, taught by a guest instructor, so the corporals and sergeants would be able to take it easy and either sit at the back of the lecture room or get some paperwork done. I was going to take the opportunity to get the report done, uninterrupted. At least, that was my plan.

I was on my way to the typewriter when Sergeant Gutta breezed by the OR counter. He told me to get all the cadets into 12 Platoon for the lecture, then disappeared into Captain Boisvert's office. Usually, lectures were given outside, under a marquee tent or on wooden benches, al fresco. Today, though, we would have to have the lecture in the barrack because it was raining again. I asked Medvescek to relay the message to the others so I could get to my report on Botosan, and sat down at the typewriter. Medvescek disappeared down the hall.

Lieutenant Katzko, the day's duty officer, then walked in and sat down on the OR bed, which was behind me and to the right. I asked him if he would help me write the report. I was confident he was very good at that sort of thing. It wouldn't be a long one, but I didn't want to miss anything. Katzko agreed, and I had just spooled a sheet of paper into the typewriter carriage when Sergeant Gutta looked in from the captain's office.

"Sergeant Fostaty, get Botosan in here—and hurry up with that report, the captain is waiting. Get it in here ASP."

Sergeant Gutta was the first person I had ever heard use that acronym for "as soon as possible." A few weeks before, when I'd heard it for the first time, I'd stood there in front of him not knowing what to do. The blank expression on my face must have been telling, because he said, "ASP—as soon as possible. Go!...Now!" Because of him, I began using it. In a few years, I would begin to hear other people use ASAP. It was Sergeant Gutta's shorthand for "drop everything else and do it now." For years, I was convinced he had coined the expression.

I hurried to get Botosan and brought him to the door of the captain's office. Captain Boisvert was seated at his desk with Sergeant Gutta standing by him. The captain looked up at us as we arrived at his threshold.

"Stand at attention," I whispered to Botosan.

He lazily put his heels together. I saluted, took a step back, and started to head around the corner to the OR to sit down at the typewriter. Botosan was going to have his ear chewed again, and with any luck, for the last time, before being shipped back to his home unit. I hoped the report I was writing would be enough to support sending him home. If I could just get it started.

As I left the captain's office, I noticed through the window a yellow pickup truck pulling up outside. Two men, a captain and a private, stepped out and climbed the three steps into the OR carrying a large cardboard box. They stopped and leaned the box against the counter. The visiting captain asked me where to go. I asked him what for, and he told me he was the explosives instructor. I stood on my toes and craned my neck to see there were rockets, mines, and grenades in the box. Some of them had orange and blue and yellow markings, meaning they were dummies. Without hesitation, I pointed him in the direction of 12 Platoon, down the hall and to the right. As I hurriedly resumed my assignment, I thought, surely they could have found a better box to transport the dummies in. Sergeant Gutta and Captain Boisvert then came out of the captain's office to have a few words with the visiting captain, but I was too concerned with getting my report done to pay any attention to what they were saying.

The explosives safety lecture the cadets would hear aimed to show what grenades, rockets, and certain types of ammunition looked like, and to discuss what these weapons were capable of and how to avoid them. In the event they came upon one in a field or on a range, they would know to leave it alone and report the sighting, so that a disposal team could retrieve it and take care of it safely. The examples they would see were inactive ordnance or dummies. Although it was unlikely, it was not unreasonable to assume that unexploded or spent ordnance could be lying around an army base; accordingly, whether live or inactive, cadets were instructed to treat all ordnance as equally dangerous.

•

I had some first-hand experience with this sort of scenario. Some years earlier, as a cadet, I attended a weekend training at Camp Farnham, a small, World War I-era camp near Montreal. Farnham was the first camp I encountered as a cadet. The mess was newish, but that was as far as any upgrades went. The barracks were wooden and painted dark green, unlike those at Valcartier, which were white on the outside. At the centre of each of Camp Farnham's long huts was an oil stove that, without a fan, somehow magically radiated heat in all directions, keeping the hut quite warm in winter. But the stove, the dark green interior, and the low ceilings gave the barracks a kind of prison camp feel.

The thing I remember most vividly about this camp was the latrines. There was no indoor plumbing in the barracks; instead, a wooden latrine hut stood across the road from each cluster of barracks. Upon entering the latrine, I was immediately struck—after the bouquet, of course—by the complete lack of privacy. Five wooden toilet seats were arranged in a row against the right wall. They were elevated a few steps, almost like bleachers, and each had a toilet paper roll on a wooden peg mounted on the wall behind. There were no dividers between the seats, which were surprisingly close together. I always felt strange and uncomfortable walking into the latrine and seeing a few folks sitting high up on the seats with their pants around their knees, engaging in conversation while fixing their eyes straight ahead, as if watching a movie screen above the urinals.

Against the opposite wall was a row of urinals, the like of which I had never seen before or since: giant metal funnels going straight into the ground, with a bowl about forty-five centimetres in diameter at the top and a backsplash plate that rose less than half a metre above the funnel and ran around the back of the urinal for obvious practical reasons. The urinals worked fine for the first little while, but whoever had designed them couldn't have taken into account the sheer volume of waste they would have to support. As the short span of a weekend elapsed, the toilets would announce the rising capacity of their foul bounty with an evil odour. The urinals, though, would be more visual in their report: they would stop draining and begin to fill. As each milestone passed through the day—breakfast, break, lunch, break, dinner, and so on—the level would rise steadily in the large bowls of the funnels until one simply couldn't relieve oneself without starting a wave that inevitably bounced off the backsplash and returned to spill ashore. As a remedy, I began to use the latrines farther down the road where the corresponding barracks were empty. It was well worth the walk.

I was returning to my barrack from the far latrine one day, walking at the side of the road in a field, when I noticed a small, red piece of metal sticking out of the ground near my feet. I kicked away at it to loosen it, then reached down and pulled it out of the ground. It was a small red and silver, rocket-shaped object with holes drilled all through it. I turned it around in my hands to inspect it and then threw it down and went on my way. I must have rubbed an eye soon after, because it started to burn so badly I couldn't see out of it for quite a while. I had to wash my eyes repeatedly to stop the burning. I shouldn't have touched that canister, of course. It was probably an old tear-gas rocket. I never told anyone about it, but I couldn't have been the only one to do something like that if it was thought necessary to create an entire safety lecture on the subject.

•

As the lecture was about to begin in 12 Platoon, I sat down and began to type. If I could finish the report in time, I might be able to catch some of the lecture, I thought. It was 1331 when I heard the chatter in the platoon die down. The lecture had begun.

While I worked at the typewriter, Lieutenant Katzko came and stood behind me, looking over my shoulder to help with wording and spelling. Botosan was still in the office with Captain Boisvert and Sergeant Gutta. Katzko and I watched Bubbles Fullum amble lazily through the gate at the counter and then drop down on the OR bed behind us. He paused only a moment before moving his feet up onto the bed and stretching out, his hands behind his head. I was almost finished the report, so Katzko announced he was going to see how the lecture was progressing. He left the OR and walked casually in the direction of 12 Platoon.

According to inquest testimonies, before the lecture began, the box of dummy explosives was supervised by a private, the ammunition technician or "ammo tech." The cadets filed quickly through the door because there were many of them and they were eager for a good spot on the floor from which they could either see well or lounge against the wall at the back. When they were all in and settled, sitting cross-legged on the floor, Captain Giroux, the guest instructor, was introduced.

The captain began to lecture the cadets on the history and inherent dangers of explosives. He explained that the items he was about to show them were all dummies and were just for display purposes. He let them know that if they ever encountered anything that resembled one of the items they were about to see, they should contact a senior officer or the police and never touch them. Some of the cadets reportedly joked and asked the captain if the items he was about to show them were armed.

"I don't want to die here,"[32] he replied.

As the captain finished describing each item, he showed it to them and then either passed it to a cadet or to the private to have it circulated around the room so that as many cadets as possible could get a closer look. At some points during the lecture, the items were getting held up at the front, where they were being more closely examined. "Captain Giroux was giving explosives to cadets in the front and was also throwing some to cadets at the back of the room."[33]

Inside the cardboard box that had been used to transport the dummies, there was a green, fibreboard container. It was a grenade container for a live M-61 grenade. It was open and it was empty.[34]

One of the cadets was passing along the plain blue dummy grenade he had been holding when he noticed his neighbour trying to get the safety pin back into a green grenade. The neighbour finally got the pin back in, but as he handed over the green grenade, he advised him not to bother pulling out the pin as it was too hard to get back in place. The cadet took the green grenade, looked at it, and passed it on. It came into the hands of a D Company corporal, "who asked the captain's assistant why it was so heavy. The latter would have answered that he had put something inside so it had the same weight as a real grenade."[35]

During the course of the lecture, one of the cadets asked the ammo tech private who was assisting about the grenade that was being passed around. The ammo tech noticed that, strangely, this grenade was green and plain and didn't have the gaudy markings of a dummy, only some writing. "But knowing that all the materiel had passed through Capt. GIROUX Jean-Claude's hands, he was certain that it was a dummy."[36] He then handed the grenade back to the corporal.

One of the cadets asked, "If a grenade exploded in this room would everybody be killed?"

"It is possible," the captain answered, "but I prefer not to think about it."[37]

Another cadet was watching the green grenade passing from hand to hand, slowly making its way toward him. He had not been able to examine anything but a .50mm bullet until now. It came to Mangos, who was beside him. Mangos half pulled the pin out and asked the instructor if it was safe to do so.

The captain answered, "Yes."[38]

While Mangos struggled to get the pin back into the green grenade, the cadet beside him, who had taken an interest in it, asked Mangos if he could have it next. Mangos had already started to pass it to Lloyd, who was on the other side of him.[39] Lloyd had a good look at the green grenade, turning it over to see the bottom of the handle.[40] It was smooth, green, unlike the others, and it had some writing on it. It also had a pin holding the safety lever in place. On the end of the pin was a ring. He put his hand on the ring to pull it out.

Mayhem

Bubbles Fullum got up from the orderly room bed and stood beside me while I typed. He stretched and yawned, then leaned on the back of my chair to read the report over my shoulder.

"How should I end this?" I asked him. He shrugged. I wanted this report to be complete and effective, and I had to get it done and into the captain's hands before he finished with Botosan. I looked at my watch—1351. "Let's go ask Katzko."

Fullum and I walked out of the OR through the swinging gate into the corridor, then down the hall, heading through the common area into the 12 Platoon barrack, when there was a sharp thump, like a large crate had been dropped on the building from up high. The noise sounded like a thunderclap without the rolling echo afterward, almost as if we were in the centre of it. The sound took me by surprise and shook the building—no, the whole company—with a shock wave. I could hear glass shatter as a window blew out, and there was a moment when everything went silent. Then, as if on cue, there were cries, and people began screaming and streaming out of the barrack through the side door—at least one person went through a window.

Bubbles and I leapt toward the 12 Platoon doorway to meet Lieutenant Katzko in the hallway, bent over clutching at his stomach as though he was hugging himself. He was moving slowly with uneven, wavering steps, and a few people bumped him as they passed on either side of us. Their hands, faces, and clothing were spattered with blood. Some had torn clothing and their eyes were filled with terror. Katzko was staring blindly ahead, his eyes wide and his mouth hanging open. He had been hit by something, but by what we didn't yet know. We lunged for him and, as he reached us, his knees buckled. His forward momentum forced us to steady ourselves with a few backward steps before he collapsed in our arms. Fullum and I just caught him before he could hit the ground.

Sergeant Gutta flew by us on his way into the barrack as we struggled to position Katzko so we could move him. Fullum and I carried and dragged him to the OR, squeezing through the gate at the counter, and laid him on the bed. I moved his hands away from his belly to see a black spot surrounded by a slowly expanding blood stain in the centre of his blue work-dress shirt. He began to force himself up but contorted his face in pain as he fell back on the cot. He told us he wanted to go back to help the cadets. There was no way; he couldn't even sit up. I told him we would take care of the others, and then turned to rush back to the platoon, leaving him in Fullum's good hands.

Something had exploded in the barrack, and I thought there might be more injuries. As I turned and took the three steps toward the counter, I ran into Botosan. He had come out of the captain's office and was standing at the gate craning his neck, trying to get a look at Lieutenant Katzko. It was a narrow passageway, and he was blocking it. I told him to get outside. He didn't move; he might have been in shock. I turned sideways and squeezed past Botosan, who still wasn't moving. I grabbed him by the arm as I went by. I wanted to get back to the barrack but I knew we would need help. So, holding Botosan's arm, I pulled him quickly through the OR door, down the stairs, and outside to the end of the OR building. I took his hand and put it on the crank of the alarm siren that hung on the corner of the building.

There was a manual crank-operated alarm siren at the end of every OR at every company. They emitted a low, plaintive moan and had all been installed that year. The old alarms were iron triangles and strikers that had been painted so many times over the years that they had become ineffective, producing only a muted thud when struck.

I started cranking the siren with Botosan's hand under mine

and told him to keep cranking until help arrived. We needed an ambulance, at least for Katzko, so I knew we needed to contact the medical inspection room (MIR) as well. It struck me then that I had to get to the MIR to have them send help. I realized in a flash that running to the MIR would be faster than searching for the number in the telephone directory in the OR.

Botosan turned the crank twice and stopped. I yelled at him to keep turning as I spun on my heels and bolted for the MIR, which was about ninety metres away. As I ran, I heard the siren stop again, but I couldn't return to spur him on. It was almost as if he read my mind, though, because the siren moaned to life once more.

I reached the back of the MIR at full speed, slamming into the bottom of the closed door. Like all the buildings at the camp, it was raised off the ground. I banged on the bottom of the door with both fists. This was the back door, and there weren't even any steps up to it. I didn't want to waste precious minutes running around the building to the front door, so I banged away on the door for all I was worth, thinking, Why the hell doesn't someone open the bloody door? At last, a medic opened up and a few of them crowded the doorway high above me looking down with expressions that spoke of surprise and condemnation.

They started to shout at me, asking what the hell I was doing banging on the door like that. My eyes were not quite level with the medics' kneecaps. I tried to make them understand that there had been an accident, an explosion, at D Company. The medic who had opened the door looked down at me as if I was crazy, and then she said they couldn't help me because there was an emergency at D Company. I was stunned for a second, until I looked around her shins to see Corporal Banzal at the front door on the opposite side, obviously making the same request.

He saw me and yelled, "Gerry, it's taken care of!"

I turned and started to run back to the company. A sudden thought hit me like a hammer: Oh God, Nick!

My brother was in that room. I had completely forgotten him in the chaos of the crisis. I started running faster and faster until I couldn't feel my legs any longer. I reached the company and ran around the end of the orderly room, noticing that Botosan was no longer at the siren. There were a few people standing about or sitting on the ground looking stunned and confused. I headed for the side door of the 12 Platoon barrack. A cadet limped past me in the opposite direction, while another lay on the ground staring down at the moist sand. It had stopped raining, and in the thick, wet air a brown smoky haze was rolling out of a broken window and through the open door.

I leapt up the three steps into the room and looked around, getting my eyes adjusted to the dim light and the smoke. I was completely unprepared for what I saw.

Through the dense, acrid smoke, I could make out a large black burn hole in the floor, and people lying all around. Some were moving, others were not. The few who were moving were helping those lying on the floor or crying and moaning and calling for help. I saw Paul Wheeler kneeling over someone on the floor. Blood was spattered and smeared on the walls. I couldn't see Nick anywhere.

I looked around to try to decide what to do first, but I had no idea where to start. A cadet stood up and came two steps toward me. He was shaking violently and his left arm was covered in blood. He stopped right in front of me and just blankly stared at me, so I walked him outside where he could be taken care of. There were others just outside the door now, getting people to safety, away from the building, so I handed him off. I quickly glanced around for any sign of my brother as I ran back up the steps and into 12 Platoon.

Whatever had happened could happen again, I thought. We had to get everyone out right away. As I cleared the threshold again, I saw Paul looking in my direction, but I don't think he saw me. He was busy with someone else who was injured. He must have been readying people to be taken out. I couldn't get to him, though, to help him move the person he was tending to—there were too many people covering the floor between us. I hastily scanned the room for someone else to move and for any sign of my brother. No Nick.

There was confusion and panic, shouting and chilling cries and moaning as people waited to be helped out of the barrack. I still had no idea what had happened. I noticed a bloody handprint smeared on the wall as the RSM came up the stairs behind me and walked past me into the barrack. There was no use trying to decide who was most in need. So many were lying on the floor that we would have to remove people to create a pathway anyway.

One cadet stared at me as I moved toward him. I could see through the rip in his pants that he had a leg injury, but I didn't think it would keep him from walking with assistance. As I bent over to help him up, I saw the cadet just behind him, about a metre away. I felt my stomach jump. His face was gone. There was no way I could have said who he was, because the front of his head was a mass of red pulp.

I turned my attention to the injured cadet in front of me, helped him up, put his arm over my shoulder, and walked him straight out the door. As I steadied him down the steps, he tried a few times to look back into the room. I twisted my body to keep him from turning around. I didn't want him to see the boy behind us. Once outside and down the steps, I helped him limp around to the front of the company by the orderly room. I found a folded stretcher lying on the ground and had him lean on the building as I kicked the brackets on the stretcher to unfold it. I eased him down onto it, trying to swing his injured leg gently into place on the stretcher.

A green army ambulance drove up over the uneven ground and bounced to a stop near us. It then backed in right beside us and squeaked to a halt with its big red cross on the white square directly behind me. The medic on the passenger side rolled down the window and, over his right shoulder, threw two first-aid kits to the ground beside me. He then rolled up the window and lit up a cigarette. I remember thinking, Why don't they get out and help? There were injured, bleeding, and dying people littering the ground all around the ambulance. Did they think this was a training exercise?

Karl Medvescek knelt down beside me as I stretched my arm for a first aid kit on the ground, just at the limit of my reach. "Have you seen Nick?" he asked as I tore it open.

"No, have you seen Ingo?"

"He's on the road with Nick," he said. I couldn't believe my ears. "Go see him."

I didn't hesitate. "Take over," I said as I pressed the first aid kit into his hands and ran for the road.

I could see them in the distance as I rounded the end of 10 Platoon at full speed. Nick was there with the rest of the company who were uninjured, perhaps twenty or thirty of them. They looked confused and worried, but they were calm and they were safe. They watched me anxiously as I ran toward them. "Just stay here," I said to them as I stopped. "You'll be safe here."

This spot on the road was the fire control point, where we were all trained to meet in the case of a fire or disaster. I took Nick in my arms, and we hugged for our lives. I could feel him begin to cry silently into my shoulder.

"You're okay," I whispered in his ear, while thinking to myself, He's okay. Beside him was Harold Scott, a cadet from my platoon and originally from my home unit. "Scott, please keep an eye on him," I said. "I have to go. And Nick, keep an eye on Scott!" I was already running again.

A fire truck whined ahead of me as I ran back around 10 Platoon to the end of the OR where I had left Medvescek. I heard someone yell for stretchers just as I returned. Medvescek had moved on and the ambulance was gone, but a small three-quarter-ton truck stood in its place. Its tailgate was down and the back was full of folded stretchers. I began unloading them as fast as people could pick them up. Once an unloaded pile had accumulated, I grabbed a stretcher and began to look for someone to put on it. I didn't have to go far.

George Mawko was reclining on his elbows on the ground under the hand-crank siren a few yards away, his face twisted in a shocked smile. I asked him where he was hurt. He said nothing but pointed to his foot. Part of his boot had been torn by shrapnel, and blood was seeping steadily through the hole. I kicked open the stretcher and placed it beside him. At once, he used his arms to lift himself up and onto the stretcher, wincing with the pain of putting even a small amount of weight on his injured foot. I carefully moved his feet onto the stretcher. Fullum then came over and dropped to his knees beside me. Fullum decided that Mawko's boot had to come off so that we could apply a dressing to stop the bleeding. We needed something to cut the laces to get the boot off, so we both sprinted toward the OR to look for scissors, leaving Mawko behind.

People were scattered all over the sandy, wet ground outside the OR building, weeping, screaming, and bleeding. To get to the OR door, we had to run around them as though in a labyrinth. The other NCOs were trying their best to ready everyone to be evacuated, placing them on stretchers where they could be easily accessed by the ambulances that were starting to increase in frequency.

As Fullum and I cleared the OR threshold, Sergeant Gutta was on his way out and yelling at Botosan to get outside. I couldn't understand why Botosan had gone back into the building, but I was too busy to linger over the thought. We frantically searched through the drawers, shelves, and counters but couldn't find scissors anywhere. Fullum then yelled that he had found a carpet knife, and we rushed back outside.

When we got back to Mawko, less than a minute after we had left him, we found he had been moved about three metres to make room for more stretchers. Fullum kneeled down and, with the blade edge facing upwards, started to rip through the laces. He had a dressing ready to apply, so I thought I would see what I could do for someone else. Fullum agreed. "Okay, I'm fine here, go," he said.

I stood up and turned to see Bob Gibeault about nine metres away, standing over a stretcher at the edge of the crowd and looking around for someone to help him with it. We caught each other's eye, and I headed over to him. As the injured were evacuated from the building, they were being placed on the stretchers on the sand outside. Because of the urgency to get them to safety in case there was another explosion, there was no order to the way they were being placed on the ground. It was more important to get them outside and out of danger than it was to organize their positions on the sand. Consequently, the pathways between the stretchers were disappearing, making it impossible to get from one point to another in a straight line.

I ran through the maze of stretchers to get over to Gibeault, sometimes having to run away from him to get closer to him. It was almost like a bad dream, but I had to run carefully, knowing that, if I tripped, I would most certainly fall on top of someone who was injured. Upon reaching him and without a word, I took one end of his stretcher and he took the other, and we laboured toward an ambulance parked nearby, trying to keep from stepping on the injured boys and prevent the cadet on the stretcher from falling off.

The cadet was shrieking that he couldn't see and was thrashing his arms around. He was an anglophone! I didn't recognize him, yet I knew that all the English-speaking cadets were in my platoon. I had to rely on his voice to try to make out who he was, because his hair was wet and matted with blood and his face was almost completely masked with dirt and blood. Blood was coming from his mouth, too. It looked as though some of his teeth were gone. As he shrieked, I thought I saw another one come tumbling out.

"Lift it higher," said Bob, wanting to keep the stretcher from bumping the people who were on the ground.

"Okay, I'm trying," I answered, struggling to get it higher.

"Sergeant!"

My God, it was Malcolm's voice. It was Malcolm. It couldn't be. Malcolm didn't look like that.

"Sergeant Fostaty! Is that you?!"

"Malcolm, yes."

Bob had the front end of the stretcher, so he climbed backward up the steps into the ambulance as we slid the stretcher in on the right side. I tied the back of the stretcher down to the stays while Bob tied down the front end.

"Okay, my end is in," I said.

"Sergeant, I can't see! I can't see! Help me!" He was pleading and crying.

I didn't know what to say to him. I couldn't help him. My mind was reeling.

The RSM then came up behind me, clearly agitated. He was speaking French so quickly that I couldn't make any sense of what he was saying. From his hand signals, though, I could see that he wanted me out of the ambulance. I jumped down and yelled to Bob, who was still inside the ambulance, to take care of Malcolm. There was no need for me to say that, other than to let Malcolm know there was still someone in there with him and that he would be taken care of. He was crying in gasps as someone loaded another stretcher into the ambulance, this time on the left side.

On this new stretcher was his buddy, Mangos. He was quiet. He wasn't moving. As they slid the stretcher in, I saw that Mangos's eyes were closed. His neck was split, but there was very little blood. I began to feel my body shake, knowing that there was nothing more I could do for them. I took a step backward away from the ambulance as the back doors were slammed shut, and the latch squeaked into the lock position. Even now, Mangos and Malcolm were together. I watched the green ambulance bounce away over the bumpy ground as something hit me in the shoulder, wrenching me around. It was the RSM, who just walked away in a daze.

I turned back again to watch the ambulance swing right past 10 Platoon as it headed toward the road up to the hospital. All around me on the ground, stretchers were filled with the wounded and weeping. The ambulances would have to keep coming and coming until, at last, the crying stopped.

We continued evacuating those still inside. As I got someone to safety or dressed a wound or moved a stretcher, I felt both powerless and anxious that I was missing something else more important or someone more in need. The mayhem seemed to go on for the longest time, but I was told later that it was only a matter of around fifty minutes.

We NCOs hardly spoke to each other during the confusion, not because we knew what to do—this was as foreign to us as anything could be—but because we were all operating on autopilot, fuelled by adrenaline. We were responsible for the safety and well-being of our cadets, and I felt I was failing them with each step because I couldn't help them or protect them. While I was engaged with one person, I was always feeling, what else, where else, who else? No matter what we did, the boys were still afraid—some were wounded and some dying. Few dressings were available, and no one appeared to be in charge. We all thought someone would sort it out at the other end.

Finally, the last of the injured was taken away, and everything seemed to begin to slow down. Nothing was moving around me as I stared expectantly at the 12 Platoon doorway, ten metres away. Everyone, those few of us who remained, stood perfectly still. I was standing next to a fire truck, strangely mesmerized by the purr and the smell of the diesel engine behind me. Then, a firefighter came into my field of vision, startling me. He asked me what had happened. I said, truthfully, I didn't know.

He asked, "How many dead?" I had heard someone say seven earlier, so I told him that.

"Oh God," he said, "just kids."

It all seemed to end as abruptly as it had started. I was looking around for the next calamity to strike. I felt as if I had been punched repeatedly in the dark, and now the punching had stopped. I was tensed for the next blow, but it didn't come. Still buzzing with adrenaline, my attention was pulled to my right. Banzal was standing a few metres away at the other end of the fire truck. He suddenly and quietly began to sob, trying to hide his anguish by looking down at the ground. I put my arm around his shoulders, a feeble gesture. I wanted to cry with him, but there were no tears. Not yet.

Aftermath

The rest of the company, those who had not been injured, were still around the corner at the fire control point on the road, about fifty metres away, waiting. Sergeant Gutta told us to get them to the kitchen, which meant the mess, so a few of us went to the road. They were all still there, looking at us expectantly as we approached. They had only a few questions — they must have known we didn't have answers yet. We told them we would let them know more when we did. We formed them up and marched them to the mess. We could have walked, but marching was the normal thing to do, and I think we all needed to feel a bit normal. So we marched, but no one called the cadence.

On our way up the road toward the mess, I noticed Paul Wheeler some distance off to my left, slowly walking between the buildings in the same direction we were. He was taking the shortcut we had taken to breakfast that morning. I called out to him a few times but he didn't seem to hear me. He just looked straight ahead and kept on walking parallel with us.

We met up with Paul when we arrived at the mess. I said a few words to him, but again he didn't answer. He didn't even turn toward me when I spoke. I found out later that his hearing had been impaired by the blast. It slowly came back as the day progressed.

It was in-between mealtimes, so we were able to get the cadets into the mess and seated very quickly. While we waited for Sergeant Gutta to arrive with instructions, the mess was eerily quiet. Moments later,

Gutta came in and picked a spot about fifteen metres off to the side where he could survey the whole group. He held up his clipboard.

"Porte attention! Listen up!" He boomed. "Answer when your name is called!" Everyone turned to face him as he took the nominal roll. There were many more moments of silence than "Here, Sir"—I counted seventeen in my platoon, the hardest hit.

Some of the white-clad civilian kitchen staff silently offered us cups of tea and stared at us in amazement. They weren't expecting anyone here at this time of day. They didn't know what had happened. No one did. Their manner, though, suggested they knew something serious was up. Perhaps they were reading the grimness in our faces. Some cadets just stared into space. Some tried to hide that they were crying. Others played tic-tac-toe, and one even attempted quietly to sing. The hot tea gave me something to focus on and allowed me to look around, slowly, over the cup as I sipped. I was trying to make sense of what had happened and what would happen now. I was waiting for instructions from Sergeant Gutta. His strength and directness were holding me together. I was ready to do whatever he said.

I saw him making notes after he called the roll. Then, he straightened out his papers in his clipboard and said to me, "I'll be back," and hurried off.

Now what? I knew though, that when he came back, there would be a plan.

I had a sudden attack of panic. Where was Engels? I couldn't remember his name being called or his response to his name. I had spoken briefly to Engels's mother before he arrived at the base that summer. She asked me if I thought he would be okay. Sven Engels was from my home unit, and his mother was a bit apprehensive about his being here. I thought she was being overprotective, but I assured her it would be a great experience and he would be fine. Now all this had happened, and I couldn't see him . . . Ah, there he is! Thank God.

We languished in the mess for about an hour, the rain pounding on the roof above us, until some transport trucks arrived and we loaded the cadets onto them. They were being transported to the big base theatre to watch a movie; some of them would be treated in the theatre lobby for ringing ears and minor scrapes. Everyone who had been in the room during the explosion would be examined. As I had only been on my way to the room, that did not include me.

It looked to me that we were being kept occupied for two reasons. First, constant forward motion might keep the cadets' minds busy and off what had just happened. Second, and more important, we were to be separated from the other companies. The cadets were huddling in twos and threes, quietly discussing what they knew and slowly piecing together the puzzle of what had happened.

The trucks stopped outside the theatre, the tailgates were swung down, and we dismounted. We hurried inside to avoid becoming drenched in the rain. The movie featured sword fights, chariot races, and women in slinky Roman costumes. It was an effort to pass some time, I guess, and a distraction.

The general consensus of those who had been in the room was that either a grenade or an anti-personnel mine had exploded. As the cadets sat waiting for the movie to roll, they talked animatedly, speculating and arguing over what caused the blast. I overheard them say that dummy grenades and mines had been passing around when something went off. Then someone said the captain giving the lecture had been holding a mine in his hands and describing it.

The talk stopped as the theatre lights dimmed and the opening titles appeared on the screen. It seemed to me that the sound was a bit too loud—perhaps it was just that there were fewer people in the theatre than usual and fewer bodies to baffle the sound, but it might have been turned up to discourage talking.

We NCOs stood in the dark at the back to keep an eye on things while the cadets watched the movie. With my hands clasped behind me, I soon noticed that they felt sticky. I couldn't see them in the dark, so I headed to the washroom to clean them. When I got into the light, on the stairs, I saw that my hands were marked with patches of reddish-brown dried blood, now getting tacky in the heat of the theatre. I bolted down the stairs to the lobby, past the cadets who were being examined, and dashed outdoors. I began to rub my hands vigorously on the wet ground; then, realizing what I was doing, I stood up, embarrassed. I was relieved no one had seen me. I walked briskly to the washroom to clean off.

Dried blood doesn't wash off very easily, especially with the liquid soap in a theatre washroom. There seemed to be no hot water either, which made the task even more onerous. I was impatient to get the blood off my hands and had to use my fingernails to scratch away the more stubborn spots. When I was finished, I looked at my hands and couldn't decide whether they were pink from being lightly stained by blood or from the harsh scrubbing and scratching in cold water. I felt I wanted to hide them. I couldn't put them in my pockets, naturally, so I held them behind me as I made my way back into the lobby. I felt very conspicuous.

Major Brochu, our company commander, pointed at me from across the lobby and then at Bob Gibeault who was on the other side of the lobby. That got our attention. He began patting himself on the head—the hand signal to let us know he wanted us—so we hustled over from our different corners of the lobby. As Bob and I reached him, he said, "Stay close to me." He began looking around over our heads as if searching for someone.

"We are getting ready to go to the hospital," he added, looking back at us. I guess he must have read our puzzled looks because he informed us that we, the platoon sergeants, were to confirm the identity of the deceased cadets. He wanted to leave as soon as possible; he was just waiting for Daniel Seguin to show up.

I hadn't really thought about those who had died. Even though someone had mentioned it earlier, and I had relayed the information to a firefighter, it had not fully registered that there had been deaths. Major Brochu had clearly said deceased cadets, so now I knew there was more than one. We didn't see Seguin anywhere, so I offered to go and find him.

Brochu snapped, "No, I want you both here. Send someone else to look for him."

He wasn't taking any chances on our getting lost, so we sent a few people in search of Seguin. We were about to leave with Paul Wheeler, a corporal in Seguin's platoon, in his stead, when Seguin appeared, so we told Paul we would be back soon and crammed into a blue Dodge Duster to speed toward the hospital.

Major Guy Boisvert, the camp second-in-command, was sitting in the front passenger seat. He wrenched himself around to face us.

"There will be reporters at the front gate or near the hospital," he said. "You are only to say that you are emergency blood donors," he added. Then he arched his eyebrows very high. "Is that clear?"

"Yes, Sir."

•

Looking back now, I know it was probably around 1700 hours when we arrived at the base hospital parking lot. I hadn't thought to look at my watch, and the sky was heavily overcast, so there was not even a view of the sun's position to cue me as to what time it was.

We successfully avoided the press, but I did have some trouble getting into the hospital itself. In the car, I had been discreetly handling a penny, flipping it between my fingers as a distraction. As we left the car and crossed the small parking lot to get to the front door of the hospital, I dropped the coin. It hit the ground and began to roll away from the door, and I went after it. I had been trailing at the back of the group, and no one had noticed that I had momentarily turned the other way. I should have let the penny go, but I didn't. Not that I'm stingy, but I wanted to keep the only thing I had available as a distraction. It didn't take long to trap the coin with my boot and pick it up. I turned around to join the others; they were already inside and out of sight. I ran to the door and pulled it open, expecting to catch up with them, but I couldn't see past the two-hundred-and-fifty pound Military Police sergeant blocking my path. He towered over me and my eyes were level with his embroidered name tag. Martel it read. Before I could even open my mouth, he spun me around, took me by the epaulets, and not too gently, hauled me at high speed to the hospital's front desk.

"Doctor, he tried to sneak in," he boomed to a man standing with his back to us. The doctor, a captain, turned.

"What business have you here?" he began. His formality stunned me for a second.

"Sir, I came for the identification," I said quietly. Other doctors, nurses, and hospital workers nearby were turning their attention to the commotion, of which I was the focal point.

"You lost your identity card?"

"No sir, I . . . " I wasn't sure where to begin. I started to tell him everything, then realized he probably didn't need to know everything, so I began again, trying to summarize why I was there. I was looking for a flicker of understanding from the captain as I threw facts at him. He looked at me incredulously, so I became more nervous and began to stumble over my words.

Thankfully, just then, Major Boisvert came around a corner looking for me. "It's okay, Captain; he is with me."

We quickly caught up with Gibeault, Seguin, and our officers. They looked at me with both irritation that I had kept them waiting and disappointment that I had shown up, therefore propelling us closer to what we had to do. I looked at Bob and Daniel and wondered if my expression was as telling as theirs. As we stood in the hallway, I became very anxious and began to feel cold and shivery. The hospital was air-conditioned, my bush jacket was damp from all the rain, and the incident at the front door hadn't helped either. My heart was still beating like a jackhammer.

We were brought to a small room to wait. Inside, it was bare except for nine grey metal chairs lining three walls. Daniel, Bob, and I stood in the centre of the room for a while, then an officer motioned with flapping hands for us to sit down. We sat and waited, the officers standing outside the door to the room, for what seemed a long time. No one spoke.

Then a doctor came into the room, his hands in the pockets of his white lab coat and a stethoscope spilling out of the left pocket. We started to rise but he told us to stay seated. He took his time looking each of us squarely in the eyes. He then quietly and gently told us that we were going to do something we had never done before. He told us not to be frightened and that we should not cringe at what we would see.

"Do not feel sorry for the bodies," he said. "They are dead and feel absolutely no pain."

Bob Gibeault was the first to go with the doctor. He took what seemed like a long time. My imagination was fuelled by images from movies and television. I had visions of a large sterile room with stainless steel tables and refrigerated drawers.

The doctor came back alone. Seguin was taken next, but before he left he turned his head, cast a look of despair my way, and then followed the doctor. I sat there alone in that little room feeling anxious and strained. My heart pounded so hard that I could feel my head bob with every beat. The clock on the wall was ticking but the hands didn't seem to move. The ticking became louder and the pounding within my chest grew stronger as I sat there, helpless. At length, I realized the doctor had returned to the room and was standing silently in the doorway before me. He paused for a moment as I looked at him. Then he took one hand out of his lab coat pocket and, with a very small gesture, motioned for me to come to him. I walked toward him, expecting him to turn and lead the way but he didn't move.

"Sergeant," he said quietly, "I want you to look closely at the body and try to remember his name." The doctor appeared tired, and sighed after each remark. "If you don't know or can't remember, that is fine. Just don't give us any name unless you are sure." He paused. "We don't want to call the wrong boy's parents to say that he is dead." He paused again. "Well, there could be problems."

I don't know why he thought he had to explain that to me. Then he asked me if I could do it. There was no way I could have uttered a word.

I didn't even want to open my mouth for fear of what would come out; so I nodded, trying to look unaffected by the panic raging inside me. That seemed to be enough for him. He turned, and I followed.

We left the room, and he led me down a short hall. The doctor was very tall and slim and took long, slow strides. I couldn't keep in step with him, and my shorter strides made me feel like a child following behind. We came to a hallway junction and stopped in front of a closed door at one of the corners. He paused for a moment with his hand on the door handle. Then he opened the door as wide as it would go. The room, with its banks of fluorescent lights above and the stark white walls, was far brighter than the hallway.

"It is the one on the far left," he said quietly. He moved aside and held the door open with his back to let me pass.

It was nothing like I had imagined. The room was a plain rectangular box, completely bare except for five sheet-covered stretchers lying on the floor before me, a row of two along one wall, a row of three along the other, together filling almost all the space in the room. They were the same green field stretchers onto which we had loaded the cadets at the company.

The sheets did not conceal the fact that there were bodies under them, and I moved cautiously between the stretchers so as not to touch them. Once white, the sheets were now spotted and drenched with dark, drying blood. Some had dripped on the floor, and a dark red pool lay in the pathway between the stretchers. The pool was too wide to step over, and it felt slippery and dangerous underfoot, so I walked carefully through it, the blood coming partway up the soles of my boots.

On the other side of the pool, I took a few steps to reach the last stretcher on the left as instructed. A man dressed all in white—he might have been an orderly or a nurse—who had been standing with his back to the wall at the far end of the room, bent over to unveil the face and neck to just halfway down the torso of the body beneath. He then stood up and faced me, his back to the wall.

I could see clearly that the top of the boy's torn light green shirt was reddish brown with drying blood. Below, the abdomen had been blown open. I quickly moved my eyes to his face and held my gaze there. It was virtually unmarked except for tiny flecks—tiny short lines, really—of dried blood. The boy had sandy-coloured hair. His face was grey and lifeless, and his mouth was slightly open. I had seen him before, but I didn't know him. I turned my head to look back at the doctor, who was still standing by the door. He looked back at me in anticipation. I slowly shook my head.

The doctor nodded and made a sweeping motion with his arm that I took to mean I should leave the room. As I reached down for the sheet to cover the body again, I looked once more at the face. I struggled to remember his name, but he wasn't from my platoon, and I knew only a few cadets from the other platoons by name. The man in white reached over for the sheet, but I took the edge of it first. I gently covered the boy's face again. I was struck by the thought that I was the last person to attempt to identify this cadet. Gibeault and Seguin had been here already, and we had all failed to put his name to his face. It would mean they would have to wait until everyone was located and identified to confirm his identity.

I turned to walk back to the door and suddenly became aware of the number of people in the room. I had been so engrossed in what I had to do that I hadn't noticed the crowd of nurses, doctors, and orderlies leaning against the wall by the door. They were shoulder to shoulder, looking at me. I couldn't understand why they were there. I felt exposed and vulnerable as I tried, once again, not to bump the stretchers that were so close on either side of me, or to slip in the blood as their eyes followed me out of the room.

When I reached the doctor, he solidly took me by the arm and asked if I was all right. What must I have looked like? My dignity hurt, I quickly answered a shaky, "Of course."

We left the room, and across the hallway I saw someone piling up a tower of green stretchers against the wall. There were other towers farther up the hallway—there must have been sixty or seventy stretchers, at least. I hadn't noticed on the way in, but there were blood spots and many hairline-thin trails of blood on the shiny floor, all the way down the hall and arcing around the corner toward the emergency entrance. We were going the other way, toward the main entrance. I glanced back toward the door we had just left to see bloody bootprints leading in our direction. They were darker at the door and faded to nothing as they came toward us. I hadn't noticed them on the way into or out of the room. With a jolt, I realized they were mine.

●

The officers and doctors were in a close huddle, murmuring and nodding with their heads down, while I stood at the hospital's main reception desk. Someone handed me a cup of coffee as I moved next to Bob and Daniel, far enough away from the officers that we couldn't hear what they were saying. We said nothing to one another. The coffee was in a thin, beige plastic cup with a weave design on it. The cup was so thin that I had to keep switching it from hand to hand to keep from burning my fingers; even getting it close to my lips to blow on it felt dangerously hot. It had the lean aroma of machine coffee and powdered whitener.

The officers and doctors came out of their huddle, and before I could even cool the coffee down enough to get a mouthful, Major Brochu said, "Okay, let's go. Hurry and drink that coffee, Sergeant," which really meant, we're leaving right now—forget the coffee. In my haste to comply, I took a quick drink, which I immediately regretted. My throat scalded, I left the cup on the reception desk and hurried outside, determined not to be separated. I once again squeezed into the back seat of the Duster and we headed back to the theatre. I looked around as we left—I didn't see anyone from the press.

Paul Wheeler met us in the theatre lobby and told us trucks were on the way to transport the cadets back to the mess for something to eat. Cheering erupted upstairs in the theatre—evidently, the movie had just ended. The cadets soon rumbled down the theatre stairs and were directed out into the parking lot, where they stood and sat around outside on the curb for about fifteen minutes, talking about the film and seeming to avoid the events earlier in the day. Their spirits were somewhat uplifted or else they were gratefully distracted. It had stopped raining, but the sky was still grey and threatening.

I moved to the other side of the driveway to distance myself from everyone else. I wanted time to think. So much had happened in a short while, and we had been moved from place to place, and I really hadn't had time to take stock. Every time I stood still, it seemed someone was either requesting or commanding me. As I stood apart from the group, I could see it as a unit; I wanted to observe its dynamic for a while, before someone noticed me.

It didn't take long. One of my cadets, Wade, unhurriedly wandered over the driveway and spoke to me. "Most of the cadets are all right now," he said, matter-of-factly. "As far as I can see everything is under control."

I noted that he had taken the situation in hand, assessed it, and was making a report. I thought I should say something, so I thanked him. He paused, while looking me directly in the eye and said, "Sergeant, did it really happen?"

He didn't wait for a reply, but walked away, back across the driveway to the group. I am glad he did. I couldn't have answered him. I was having trouble processing it myself.

"The deuces are here!" someone yelled as the six-wheel-drive, two-and-a-half-ton transport trucks rumbled into the parking lot and squeaked to a halt in a line. The cadets were formed up into platoons to be loaded in an orderly fashion. The drivers swung down the tailgates of the six-wheel-drive transport trucks, and the cadets and NCOs climbed in, eighteen at a time. There weren't enough trucks for the entire group so they had to come in relays. I decided to wait until the last group was in the last truck before getting on — NCOs were always the last on, and would sit at the tailgate. Finally, we were all ready to go except for a lone dissenter, a cadet named Alain Couture. I stood behind the truck as he yelled he wasn't getting on anything made by the army. He was unmovable. After a few minutes of quiet conversation with him, I still couldn't convince him to climb aboard, so Major Boisvert intervened, saying he would take care of things. I got in, the driver swung up the tailgate, we secured it, and the truck lurched off, leaving Boisvert and Couture behind. As we bounced away down the road, I watched Boisvert talking to Couture for a few seconds before the two of them headed for the blue Duster.

After the three- or four-minute ride, which we probably could have walked in five, the trucks stopped in front of the mess. The cadets jumped down and we hustled them into the NCOs' mess—I think the idea was to keep them apart from everyone else. A corporal I recognized from F Company was leaving. He stopped, clapped me on the shoulder, and said, "Bonne chance, mon ami." He obviously had some idea of what had happened today. I wanted to ask him what he had heard. Instead, I stood there, speechless, as he walked away.

The clang of a truck tailgate banging home and the sound of a chain securing it brought my attention back. I turned to see the last cadet disappear into the mess and heard the last truck rumble away when I realized it was raining again. I slipped my beret off as I crossed the threshold and stood inside the mess door with my face wet. From there I could see the NCOs' mess and some cadets. Only 12 Platoon was there. Paul Wheeler and Tony Snopek, its corporals, were among the group. I couldn't grasp where the rest of the company was. I shook the excess water off my beret, then dried my face with its lining.

Paul had his harmonica out. He had intended to learn to play it this summer, but I don't remember ever hearing him practise with it; he just seemed to be able to play it from the first time I had seen it in his hands. He began playing now and a few people began to sing along, quietly and tentatively: "Les chevaliers de la table ronde, Allons voir si le vin est bon…"

I walked around the behind the group and stood by a garbage can. Looking down into it, I noticed a pair of rolled-up puttees sitting on top of the pile. I reached down and fished them out. I took the opportunity between songs to hoist them over my head and ask loudly, so everyone could hear, "Who has lost a pair of puttees. Qui a perdu ses puttées?"

Tony, horrified, hissed from the other side of the mess, "Put them back, they've got skin on them!"

I shivered, feeling my hand tighten as the rose-coloured water drained out of them, leaving a trail of pink running down my arm to my elbow. I was frozen in disbelief for a second, but then I hurled them back into the can, where they unrolled. Sure enough, Tony was right. They were shredded and there were waxy pieces of what looked like flesh on them. I turned to look back at Tony. He was still looking at me, but everyone else was otherwise occupied. I tried to look apologetic, while he looked back at me impassively.

Although the cadets had been brought to the mess for a meal, no food service was scheduled at that time. It didn't seem to matter, though, as everyone was content to sit and lose themselves in their own thoughts. I was pondering the whereabouts of my own platoon when I heard a door slam behind me.

Sergeant Gutta came into the mess, slapping his beret on his leg to shake off the rain. He walked directly to one of the tables at the end of the room, away from the cadets, and quickly sat down to arrange his papers. Then he stood up and bellowed, "Porte attention! Listen up!" The room went silent except for the drone of the kitchen exhaust fans.

"Answer when your name is called." He sat down again, but with his back to the table while he faced the cadets, and held his clipboard to reference his notes. I sat down next to him and fixed my eyes on the papers while he called the roll again. He went down the complete company list, calling all the names. My eyes followed as he moved through the list. He came to Lloyd and there was a red line under it. He called it out anyway. There was no response. I looked up at him to try and read his expression. Nothing. Then he came to Malcolm and called it. There was a red line under it, too. Again, no response. Then he came to Mangos. There was a circle around his name and beside it was marked, Décedé. I felt my throat tighten and my stomach fall. He called out Mangos's name. There was no response. I glanced up at

Sergeant Gutta, trying not to look alarmed. Neither his face nor his voice gave anything away—he was a tower of strength and control.

I looked out at the cadets, who were all looking in our direction. They were oblivious to what was tearing me apart as I listened to Gutta while he continued without pausing. I saw a few more names underlined in red. He called out the names of the entire company even though only 12 Platoon was here in the mess.

"As you were! Autant!" he called out to the group. Turning his head toward me, he said quietly, "I am going back."

"Where?" I asked him.

"To the chapel, where the rest of the company is," he answered, his head down. He made some notes and then began looking through his papers. Some people, junior officers among them, came running in out of the rain. The door slammed behind them.

"There is your temporary platoon commander while Lieutenant Katzko is in hospital," said Sergeant Gutta, indicating the clutch of incoming officers with a sideways incline of his head. He never took his eyes off his paperwork. "Go over and introduce yourself."

I went over to meet them. I recognized Rick Juneau right away. Rick had been a corporal with me the year before, when I was a corporal at H Company, but he obviously had been awarded a commission and been promoted to second lieutenant. We had been friendly the year before when he was still an NCO, so I was comfortable as I briefed him with as much detail as I could, while I kept an eye on Sergeant Gutta on the other side of the mess. When Gutta headed for the door with his paperwork secured under his arm, I told Juneau I'd see him later and went at a run after the sergeant, slipping my beret on as I left the mess.

It was starting to get dark and was raining rather hard again, so we ran the short distance to the chapel. We entered the building by way of the darkened padres' offices, closest to the mess, and went into the sanctuary. It had been transformed. The sanctuary no longer looked like a church but a huge barrack. The pews had been removed to make room for bunks, which filled the entire chapel in neat rows. The altar had been pushed up against a wall, and huge canvas bags filled with blankets and pillows placed in front of it. Extra mattresses and clean sheets were piled up neatly nearby. I was told that the cadets from the Physical Training (PT) Company had set up the bunks.

I wondered, Where are the cadets? Probably picking up clothing or something at the quartermaster — they wouldn't have been able to go back to the company to pick up their belongings. The company, we were told, was strictly off limits.

Night Watch

Within minutes of our arrival at the chapel, some cadets began to trickle in through the main entrance. They headed directly to their bunks. The line of cadets soon thickened and the room filled with a crowd of people. It was relatively quiet considering how many people there were in one room. Bob Gibeault came in with them, spotted me, and came over. He advised me to grab one of the unoccupied bunks before they were all taken. We wanted to sprinkle the NCOs throughout the chapel to monitor any unforeseen circumstances and as a measure of security to the others. I claimed a lower bunk in the middle of the room by throwing my damp beret onto the middle of the bare mattress.

Before long, all the cadets were in the chapel except those who had gone to the hospital for injuries. All were told to sit on their bunks and face the same direction. This way we could see who did not have a spot yet and which bunks were not spoken for. In French and English they were told that they had had quite a hectic day and that the best thing they could do would be to get some sleep. "It would also be appreciated if there was no noise," they were reminded. The cadets quietly and busily made their beds for the night and generally spoke in lowered voices. Perhaps they were quiet because they had been asked to keep the noise down, although that usually took two or more requests to make them comply. Maybe it was because they were in the chapel, but I think they were just exhausted.

Our company commander, Major Brochu, then strode in, smiling too broadly, and announced something out of the ordinary, notwithstanding that this had been an extraordinary day.

"There will be sandwiches, soup, and crackers brought over before the cadets retire," he said, loudly and proudly. I was later told that Sergeant Gutta had arranged for the food. "It will be here in a few minutes." The cadets cheered. They were hungry. Brochu looked pleased. I glanced at my watch for the first time since the explosion — 1950.

Had it really been eight hours? I figured the food would arrive in about ten minutes. Two hours later, at 2200, I started wondering where the food was.

Major Brochu returned to reassure us of a meal. "Well, gentlemen," he said loudly and in his jolliest tone. "Good old army efficiency." He was smiling like a guilty man. "Gentlemen," he said again, "somewhere between the mess and the chapel, a distance of less than one hundred yards, the food has gone missing." He held his hands up as if he were stopping traffic. "Do not despair. More is being prepared."

A few minutes later, it arrived in two olive-green Mermite cans, which were like rectangular five-gallon thermoses, accompanied by trays of cutlery, bowls, and a cardboard box full of crackers. The insulated containers were a familiar sight. Every night at about 2000 hours, there was a cocoa parade: a huge tray of doughnuts and two Mermite cans filled with hot chocolate would arrive at each company and the cadets would line up for an evening snack. This time, the Mermite cans were filled with soup. Two packs of crackers and a bowl of soup per person: a feast. The sandwiches never did arrive.

It wasn't long before the cadets were lining up with a bowl and spoon in hand and jamming packets of crackers into their pockets, while we ladled out the soup. It seemed that, just as we finished the serving line, they were starting to line up again to return the empties and prepare their bunks for lights out. It had been a long day, and their faces and heavy-lidded eyes made it plain that they were eager to have it end.

Once the lights were brought down, we NCOs were called for a briefing. In the middle of the room, in hushed voices, we were given our fire-picket duty schedule. A fire-picket's duties are traditionally to see that the fire in the stove doesn't go out and to ensure the building doesn't catch fire. This night, our instructions were to keep our eyes on the cadets and be on the lookout for anything out of the ordinary. The whole situation, of course, was out of the ordinary. I met and shook hands with my fire-picket partner. She was a francophone medic. It felt odd sharing our duties with strangers, but the fact that they were medics wasn't lost on me. She promised to return in an hour, when our duty began, and she left.

It would have been ridiculous for me to try to sleep just for an hour, so I took the opportunity to walk quietly around, listening to the sound of people trying to go to sleep. I saw their eyes watching me as I passed their bunks. I heard the hissing sound of people turning over in crisp, clean sheets and the occasional squeak of a bunk as someone tried to get comfortable in the unfamiliar surroundings. It seemed as though everyone was listening to everyone else, waiting for someone else to fall asleep first.

I heard the soft sound of sniffling from a corner away from the bunks and went to investigate. Between the pews pushed up against the wall, a cadet from one of the other platoons was quietly crying.

Whispering, I asked him, "Why aren't you in bed and asleep?"

He looked up at me suddenly. "I can't sleep." I had surprised him.

"Just hop in bed and close your eyes."

"I can't."

"Why not?"

"Because, I don't have a bed." He said it almost as an apology. There were tears on his cheeks, but he was trying to appear strong and unbothered. He must have arrived late and been overlooked. He wasn't small or delicate looking, but he must have felt so completely overwhelmed that he felt he couldn't ask for help.

"I have a bed just your size. Come on." I said.

He followed me, carrying his boots, as we snaked our way through the chapel and over to my bunk. He stood there beside me while I removed my beret from it. I jammed my beret under my web belt and draped the sheets and blankets onto the bed. Then he climbed in, asking me how I had found one so fast. I told him it was mine, but I had fire-picket duty, so I didn't need it. He closed his eyes and turned over. No goodnight and no thank you. I would have to make other arrangements for a bed later or hot-bed with the next person on fire-picket duty.

I looked at my watch. It was close enough to my duty to take over from the previous group, so I relieved them, clicked on my red-lens flashlight, and slowly walked around again, trying to be as quiet as possible. By now, there was some heavy, rhythmic breathing and less movement as I threaded my way around the chapel in the darkness.

When I finished my tour, I found myself near the Mermite cans and saw there was still some soup left. I ladled out a bowl for myself and sat down to eat it by the light of the exit sign. The soup was lukewarm now, having sat around for over an hour in the open cans. It might have been someone's idea of vegetable soup, but it was uninspired—thin and watery with little square bits of carrot in it. I was hungry, though, not having eaten when everyone else did, so I had a few more bowls, four in all. I felt better after that.

The day was beginning to catch up on me because, about fifteen minutes after I had eaten, I started to feel sleepy. Half my duty was over, so I decided to take another tour to help me stay alert. I kept my flashlight off. It was important to walk around to make sure that everything was as it should be, but I had to walk slowly, so I didn't trip over anything in the darkness, and quietly, so as not to disturb anyone or convey any sense of urgency. There had been enough urgency today.

As I came to the end of my circuit, near the front of the chapel, I heard an odd rumbling sound coming from down the darkened corridor toward the padres' offices. I went to investigate. The source of the strange noise became clear as I reached the chaplain's office. Padre Robert Baker, the Protestant chaplain, was asleep, slumped over a desk and snoring.

I had known the chaplain, Captain Baker, since I was a cadet. Padre Baker would frequently appear in the barracks unannounced, often just to say hello or to chat and make his way through, speaking to everyone. He always had a smile and never seemed to be in a hurry. Whenever I saluted him, he would return the salute as crisply as it was given, but it was always followed by a big grin. When he saluted, he always looked as if he was holding his breath. Today, he had been a major force in the hollowing out of the chapel to make room for the bunks as well as in the care and comfort of everyone here. He could be seen throughout the evening, moving from group to group, propping up sagging morale and keeping an eye on those most vulnerable. Yet he did this in the most subtle and discrete way. He had worked tirelessly all day, but the night had finally claimed him.

I quietly backed away, walked back into the chapel, and sat down at the table in the centre of the room. I was more tired than ever, and afraid to stay seated in case I fell asleep. The medic, who was also sitting there, glanced at me with an expression of boredom and condescension.

"You got any toothpicks?" I asked her.

"Toothpicks?" she repeated, placing her hand on her medipack. "What for?"

"To prop my eyes open," I said earnestly.

She rolled her eyes while exhaling through pursed lips and then turned back toward me to punctuate it with an emphatic and soundless "No."

Major Roger Guilbeault, the commander of the Support Division, walked in the open door and stood under the exit sign. I stood up to whisper *hello* to him and he told me to relax. The medic had stayed seated.

"Any problems, Sergeant?" he asked while trying to peer around in the darkened chapel.

"Yes, Sir, my platoon."

"What do you mean?" he said as he turned to face me.

"Seventeen out of forty-seven, Sir."

"Seventeen in hospital. Whew!"

"No, Sir. Seventeen here."

"Oh...," he said and then added, "you're doing a fine job, Sergeant."
I guess he thought that would make me feel a bit better.

"Thank you, Sir."

"Have you called home yet?"

"No, Sir. All the pay phones have been cut off." I had heard someone
mention that earlier.

He didn't contradict my information, but just said, "Go and phone
from the office."

"Thank you, Sir, but I still have..." I shined the red flashlight on
my watch, "ten minutes left of my duty."

"Well, in ten minutes, then."

"Yes, Sir."

"Good night, Sergeant."

He began to turn to leave, so I stopped him with, "Sir, do you know
the count...I mean, how many have died, Sir?"

"Yes."

"And who?"

"Yes." He wasn't going to offer anything more.

"Would you please tell me?"

He hesitated a moment and then, shaking his head, said, "I am
not supposed to." He stopped and looked at the medic at the table.
She looked bored and was staring off in the other direction, not
understanding our English exchange. I stood waiting. I wasn't going
to beg him or ask him again, but I knew that if I looked away for even
a second, he would just leave, so I kept my eyes on him. He turned to
look back at me and I held his gaze. It's no use, I thought, about to
concede.

He sighed and caved. "All right."

"How many?" I ventured quietly.

"Five."

"Oh, no. . ." He wasn't going to elaborate. "Who?" I prodded.

"Voisard, Provencher, Lloyd, and Mangos. I only know four
names."

"And Malcolm?" I remembered Malcolm in the back of the ambulance with Mangos.

"He's all right, but he lost an eye, I think."

"Lieutenant Katzko?"

"He's fine. Last time I saw him he saluted the colonel," he said smiling, trying to lighten the conversation. Then he asked, "Any of the cadets from your platoon?"

"Two."

"I'm sorry." He paused, looking uncomfortable. There was really nothing more that could be said. Then, he changed the subject. "Did you have any of that vegetable-flavoured water?" He pointed at the Mermite cans.

"The soup, Sir?"

"Yes." He smiled, shaking his head.

"Yes, Sir."

"I thought you looked a little sleepy," he said with a quiet smile.

"Sir?" Was he trying to change the subject again?

"Yes, a bowlful of warm soup might help you to sleep." He raised his eyebrows. "Did you have a bowl?"

"No, Sir, four."

He laughed and then caught himself and put his hand up to his mouth before he woke anyone. His quickly stifled outburst had caught the medic's attention. She turned lazily toward him, and he held up a hand as much as to say, *Yes, yes I'm going*. The medic was completely unresponsive.

"Good night, Sergeant." And then he left.

"Good night, Sir."

I looked at my watch. My duty was over. It was time to wake Seguin, who was next up. His bed was a mattress on the floor not far from the table where the medic sat. I woke him by shaking the mattress with the toe of my boot.

"Seguin...Moose, wake up," I hissed. "Lève-toi. It's your turn to take the watch." I didn't want to wake anyone else, so instead of getting louder, I attacked the mattress more aggressively with my boot.

Sleepily, with his eyes still closed, he managed a well-enunciated, "Mange la merde." With that, I slowly lifted one corner of the mattress and poured him onto the cold cement floor. He stood right up, his eyebrows arched high as though trying to prop up his sagging eyelids. I handed him the flashlight, and the next thing I knew, I was through the doors and pointed in the direction of the administration building to use the phone.

•

The whole camp was still and dark as I walked toward the admin building in the warm night. The foggy air was perfumed with the sweet, thick smell of vegetation after a heavy rain. The air was dead calm. The quiet was unsettling, broken only by the soft crunch of the gravel and sand under my boots. There was usually some kind of noise here: conversations, marching, commands being shouted, a baseball or soccer game, laughter, vehicle traffic noise. Not tonight, though. I had completely lost track of time. Even though I had looked at my watch numerous times that night, the time hadn't really registered until now. It was the middle of the night.

I saw the admin building complex in the distance. Like the other buildings on the base, it was low, narrow, and long: a series of company orderly rooms strung together in a line. All the other buildings were dark, but from the open doors and windows of the admin building streamed shafts of light, glowing softly in the damp air. A few officers were out front, just standing around in the light, one side of their bodies and faces illuminated, the other side disappearing into the shadows. A tiny red glow in front of a face traced the path of a cigarette lifted to a mouth. It was easy to tell they were officers, even at a distance. They wore dress greens or work dress; we NCOs wore bush dress. I could see through the windows that more officers were inside. Some were walking about, a few others were sitting doing some sort of paperwork. Strange for them to be working so late, I thought.

As I approached the building, all the officers out front turned toward me almost languidly. It was as strange for them to see me walking at this hour as it was for me to see them standing around outside in the dark. I slowed down as I reached the walkway leading to the front door to scan the group for Major Guilbeault, the officer who had invited me to use the phone. He was nowhere to be seen. Instead, I was met on the walkway to the door by Captain Marc Fortier. He was a short, pleasant man with a full, neatly trimmed moustache. He always seemed to have a pipe in his mouth. I recognized him, having seen him around at the camp, but I had never spoken to him. He greeted me with a warm smile as he moved down the path toward me.

I was about to explain about the invitation from Major Guilbeault when he spoke.

"Sergeant." A thin whisper of smoke escaped from his mouth as he removed the pipe from between his teeth. His smile broadened, and I saluted.

"Sir, could I..."

"Sure," he interrupted, as he threw back a relaxed salute. "What's the number?" Evidently he had been expecting me.

We went to the counter just inside the doorway to make the call. He reached far across the counter and pulled over the phone, a black, rotary dial model, and dialled the number while holding the receiver up to his ear. He continued to grin at me as he waited for someone on the other end to pick up the phone. I could just make out the *rrrrrr...* *rrrrrr* of the phone ringing at the other end.

"Mrs. Fostaty? Captain Marc Fortier from the cadet camp calling. One of your sons is here. Would you like to speak to him?"

He passed me the phone. It didn't even occur to me that it was so late on a Tuesday night, or was it Wednesday by now? She must have been in bed asleep when the phone rang. Captain Fortier moved a few steps away from the counter and half-turned to look out the doorway to give me the illusion of privacy while I spoke with my mother. I held the phone away from my ear, waiting for Captain Fortier to move away before I began to speak to her.

"Hello, Mom?"

"How are you?" she began, tentatively, with the most obvious, pressing question.

"Fine," I lied, knowing she needed to hear that. I thought I would pre-empt her next question. "We're both fine. Not a scratch on us." She was silent on her end so I said, "I can't wait to get home." In the lull, I looked over at Captain Fortier. He stood with his back to me, one hand behind him and the other on his pipe. His light green shirt was brightly lit by the lights above my head, and the inky blackness of the night framed him in the open doorway.

"How is Nick?" she asked.

"He is okay, really. He is taking it pretty well." He was, too. I had checked in with him a few times over the course of the rest of the day, as discreetly as I could, to see how he was handling the situation. He didn't seem to be showing any outward signs of stress; however, at eighteen, I was certainly no expert on the subject.

"I didn't even know it had happened until I got a call from Maurice Seguin," she said. Mr. Seguin was a neighbour. "He came over to the house to tell me. He said he saw you on TV, so he knew you were okay."

I couldn't imagine, though, how I came to be on TV. I had seen no cameras and we were isolated from the outside world in the middle of the base. I wanted to explain to my mother what had happened, but I didn't know what to say, or where to begin. I certainly didn't want to say something I shouldn't, with so many people apparently listening to my conversation. Although they were all conspicuously looking away from me, the only one moving other than me was Captain Fortier, and his only movement was when he would let a puff of pipe smoke go.

"What happened?" she asked.

"I don't really know exactly," I said. The office was dead quiet now, except for me. I could hear the crackle of the tobacco burning as Captain Fortier drew on his pipe and watched the smoke curl around his cap in the still air. I didn't go into any details with my mother but said, "Maybe when I get home on my next leave."

"Okay," she said, seeming to perceive that I was uncomfortable.

"Say hello to everyone at home for me. Bye, Mom."

"Bye, son."

She was obviously worried. She never called me son.

I thanked and saluted Captain Fortier on my way out. After leaving the admin building, I walked back to the chapel. I had to move slowly because my eyes had become accustomed to the bright light inside, and I was heading back toward a darker area of the camp. A dim light over the chapel entrance guided my return.

In the red glow of the exit sign within the chapel, I found my bed: the mattress on the floor from which I had dumped Seguin a half-hour earlier. He would have to hot-bed later that night. He was half-asleep, leaning on a table, rubbing his eyes, and clutching the flashlight. As I unwound my putties, I could see he was fighting to stay alert, as I had done earlier. He got up and began his rounds as I took off my boots and dropped my weights and putties into them to keep them from getting lost. I stretched out on the mattress.

I lay there listening to the sounds of people sleeping, Seguin's slow footsteps as he made his rounds, and some hushed whispering on the other side of the chapel. It sounded like Sergeant Gutta. As I felt my heartbeat begin to slow down, I reflected on what had happened throughout the day, on home and family, and on how I wanted to get home. I resolved to call home again in the next few days, once the pay phones were working again. I knew that if I didn't make a firm commitment to call, I wouldn't. In a few days, perhaps I would have a much better idea of what had happened, and I could tell about it in the privacy of a phone booth.

I was exhausted, yet afraid to go to sleep. I had reached my limit. I wanted it all to stop, and I wanted to go home. That's it, I would just go home. It would be easy, I thought. Tomorrow I could claim some vague symptoms of a manufactured illness and that would be it. They would have to let me go. It wouldn't be that straightforward, though, and I knew it. I intended to close my eyes only for a few seconds, but sleep consumed me.

The Days After

"Get up, Gerry. Come on, get up." Paul was kicking my feet. I bolted upright, panic gripping me. I thought I had only just closed my eyes, but I saw through the open doorway that it was light again outside.

It was still rather dim in the chapel. The lights were on, but just a few bare bulbs spaced far apart on the ceiling. The chapel windows were coloured glass that effected a low-level glow, but didn't really throw any light into the room. I suppose they were someone's idea of stained glass: geometric shapes in red, blue, and a bit of yellow, presumably suitable for any denomination worshipping there.

Paul must have thought that I was well on my way to waking, because he disappeared to start his duties. I sat on the mattress, trying to clear my head, and stared at my watch, uncomprehending. I had to say the time aloud a few times to understand what I was looking at, while my head buzzed with the sleep I still craved.

Five after six. Five–after–six. It's late! Beneath the hands on my watch it said July 31.

The chapel was beginning to stir. We were all starting to realize where we were and that this wasn't just a bad dream. I had no idea what I was supposed to do this morning. I had meant to formulate some sort of plan before going to sleep last night, but here I was, without a clue. I hoped someone else had been given some instructions. I could see the cadets were slowly getting up and dressing, but they were also looking around to see what everyone else was doing or sitting back down on their bunks to wait for someone to tell them what to do.

Now what? I wondered, as I laced up my boots and rolled on my puttes. It appeared we were on our own—no officers yet, and the medics were gone. The NCOs quickly convened, struggling to get the morning started as normally as possible. The cadets needed to be given a task to restore their sense of stability and purpose. We knew we wouldn't be going back to the company today, but might be staying put in the chapel for some time.

First, we told the cadets to make their bunks hospital-style. They took this well, believing it was easier than the evacuation-style they were used to. That ate up some time while we tried to wrap our heads around a plan for the morning. There would be no company inspection today, of course, though we didn't let the cadets know that. If this were a regular day, there would be training and classes to organize, so we decided to carry on as usual until told differently. That would at least give some structure and movement to the day. If we had to change direction, that would be easier than trying to get the ball rolling from a dead stop.

Besides the training classes and lectures, we had to ensure the cadets got a meal, perhaps fresh clothing, and settled into their stay in the chapel. Breakfast would give us more time to plan the day, and perhaps we would soon receive direction from Sergeant Gutta.

After some initial confusion forming the cadets up for breakfast parade in the absence of the usual parade square, we found a quiet spot on the road to get sorted out, and marched off quickly toward the mess. We arrived at our usual time, strangely, and other companies were coming and going as well, but we kept to ourselves. There was some hushed talk and staring in our direction, but I noticed nothing else. I wondered what they had been told and what they knew.

The NCOs hurried through breakfast, then waited at strategic points to direct our cadets back to the chapel, rather than to D Company, when they'd finished eating. We needed to know where they were at all times today. We couldn't train at our own company, either; that was still off-limits, so we had to make alternative arrangements, which proved makeshift and rustic.

Back at the chapel, we attempted to begin the training day. Someone, probably Sergeant Gutta, had had the presence of mind to bring the syllabus to the chapel, and we seized on it. Giving the scheduled courses would allow us to keep busy until the administration arrived with its plan. We spaced ourselves around the chapel to lecture without distracting one another too much. I took my group to some long benches outside, near the entrance. I was supposed to teach driver safety, and I remember we talked about traffic signs. But we all knew we were just trying to fill the time. There was much moving of benches around to ensure they were all on level ground, and then I had them moved again as the sun came up over the building to keep it out of the cadets' eyes. What I really wanted to do was sleep. The two hours I'd had that night had merely teased me; most of the cadets, I thought, felt the same.

From above came a dearth of information. We saw few camp administrative officers and were offered little direction other than to "keep on keeping on." Sergeant Gutta made us use massive amounts of creativity and bluff to keep the cadets from suspecting we were making it up as we went along. Otherwise, he said, morale would plummet and we would lose them. I had no idea what that really meant, but I didn't want to find out. The lack of information, though, left everyone to speculate about what had happened the day before. Ridiculous stories and rumours were already making their way around. One story involved a terrorist cell — this was, after all, just four years after the 1970 October Crisis, when extremists felt it necessary to murder, kidnap, and blow up mailboxes in the name of national independence, and the experience was still fresh in peoples' minds. I don't think anyone within the company took these stories seriously, but it wasn't prudent to let rumours like that ferment.

So we waited for information and guidance, and soldiered on. I remember feeling that I was the only one who didn't know anything, other than what I'd gleaned from other people's conversations. But we were all sure we would be given the plan when it was ready. Those in charge never really gave us a plan, though. Evidently concerned with other parts of the equation, they allowed us to manufacture and maintain an artificial normality. Indeed, we did such a good job keeping the company running that they forgot about us entirely.

Inside, though, each of us was hurting. I never would have exhibited my fear and distress to the others, and I am sure they felt the same. It just wasn't done. In the darkness and privacy of the night, however, or when I found myself away from anyone's sight, that was another matter. I found myself hiding in a washroom cubicle, standing and staring at the inside of the door, or walking alone somewhere in the evening, feeling completely lost in the world. I felt I might fall apart if I was alone, so I tried never to be alone.

That first day, though, out of curiosity, I decided to get to the mess by taking the long way around past D Company. I thought I might see something that would tell me what was going on, and perhaps make me feel better. Breaking through the trees between H Company and D Company, I saw that the barracks were completely surrounded by barbed concertina wire, and armed guards were posted beside jeeps labelled "Military Police." It looked very threatening. I presumed they were still trying to figure out what had happened and were taking no chances on losing or disturbing any evidence.

I slowed down so I could take in as much as possible without stopping, and I half closed my eyes so that the guards couldn't see which way my eyes were looking. But I couldn't see anything—the concertina wire had been placed in a wide perimeter around all the buildings, preventing me from even seeing 12 Platoon. Out of the corner of my eye, I saw the guards watching me. I didn't want to appear too interested or to look guilty, so I tried not to look at all as I kept on going past my own company.

•

Inquest testimony later revealed that, within the security cordon set up around D Company by the Royal 22nd Regiment of Canada—the "Van Doos"—the bomb disposal unit was trying to determine the nature of the explosion and if there was any danger of another one. Meanwhile the 5th Engineers were busy outside the barracks with minesweepers looking for any hidden danger.[41] An investigative team was also photographing the scene of the explosion. These images, thirty-six of them, are described in the inquest documents, but were withheld by DND. Apparently, among them are pictures of the exterior of the building, the cardboard box in which the dummies were transported, and some of the dummies themselves. Pictures were also taken of the anti-tank mine the captain had been holding in his hands when the explosion occurred, the complete area of the explosion, and the exact spot of the detonation. Two pictures show the windows that were broken by the blast and two others show the perforations in the walls made by metal fragments and pieces of human bone. Four pictures show pieces of human flesh found on the floor. The file has a table of contents that lists the images, but the subsequent pages are blank, with the notation at the bottom of each page, "Withheld s.16 (1)(c)."[42]

•

In early August, a few days after the explosion, I was scheduled to travel to Montreal via CFB Longue-Pointe to attend a funeral. I had forgotten about it with everything that had gone on, and was reminded of it only the night before I was to leave. The funeral was for a colleague, Claude Charbonneau, who had been hit by lightning a few days before the explosion. This was a very unusual summer.

Charbonneau was a corporal in another company. He wasn't really a close friend, but we had gotten along well when we had trained together earlier that summer during our NCO orientation, before the cadets had arrived. He had had the bunk below mine during training. I had been asked a week ago to attend his funeral as an official representative of the cadet camp, and I had agreed. Now, I was glad I had, even though I would have to supervise a group of cadets who were also making the trip. I was looking forward to seeing the Montreal skyline again and being close to home, even if only for a few hours.

The trip afforded me no escape, though. I was crammed in the back seat of a staff car with three cadets, a three-hour trip each way, broken up by an hour or so at the funeral. The ride was uncomfortable. It was a hot midsummer day, and there was no air conditioning in the black car. We couldn't have the windows down on the highway, and it was hot and stifling. As an army staff car, it didn't have a radio, either. With nothing to do but think and perspire, I brooded over my memories of the explosion and the events afterward. I didn't dare succumb to my feelings in front of the cadets, however, and all I wanted to do was get back to the distractions of the base and its daily activities.

The funeral was uncomfortable, too. We didn't know anyone there, and Charbonneau's family was too busy with relatives and friends to notice us. We stood at the graveside, saluting and sweating as the coffin was lowered into the earth. There were some odd looks from others in attendance, who wondered who we were and why we were there. We were clearly outsiders and strangers. Their looks troubled me, making me yearn all the more to get back to the camp, where I knew I belonged.

Upon our return, it took about a week and a half to begin to adjust to our new surroundings at the chapel. Then I was given a pass, so I went home on leave for the weekend, leaving behind only six people in our company, one of whom was Nick. He had been offered a pass with everyone else but had turned it down. We never discussed the reasons he decided to stay.

It was a long bus ride from the base to Quebec City and then on to Montreal. I tried to sleep, but in those days you could still smoke on buses, and I was just one row away from the smoking section, whose inhabitants seemed to think that smoking wasn't just allowed, it was required. It was like being trapped in a burning building for several hours.

I didn't know what I'd expected from the weekend at home, but I found neither comfort nor escape. I know now that I needed to talk about what had happened, but at the time I had no sense of what to say, how to begin a dialogue, or even how to begin to sort out my own thoughts and feelings. I think I hoped someone would ask me the right questions that would allow me to begin talking. I needed to start on the critical path of self-examination, but of course, I was too young to realize that.

Instead, no one at home took any interest in what had happened. The mainstream press had paid little attention to the incident, so most people were unaware of it. Those who knew something about it certainly didn't connect me with it, and I didn't volunteer any information. My mother asked about it, but she was content to allow me to brush it off as a minor incident. I don't know if she realized that it happened not near us but to us. It was probably my own bravado-fuelled fault that she didn't pursue it. Neither my father nor my sisters asked. I felt as though I was isolated in a soundproof booth, surrounded by two-way mirrors. I could see out and was expected to participate in activity and conversations, but no one could see into the booth. They were all standing on the outside, oblivious to the beating I was taking on the inside.

I felt better only when I boarded a bus to the base, this time making sure I sat as far from the smoking section as possible. When I got back, I walked over to the company and saw that the concertina wire and the guards that had surrounded D Company were gone. I went right up to the open doors of our platoon and stuck my head in to look around, but I didn't go inside. No one was there, but 12 Platoon was well under repair and almost completely repainted—the doors and windows were all open to let the paint dry.

A few days later, we finally—and, for some of us, nervously—moved back into the D Company complex. It was good to be back after the disorganized and makeshift accommodations at the chapel. The whole complex smelled of fresh paint, although only the inside of 12 Platoon had been given a fresh coat of light green. I took a stroll through the 12 Platoon barrack and saw not a trace of what had happened. The charred floor, the smell of burnt powder, and the blood on the floor and the walls were all gone.

Although nothing was ever said outright, it was assumed that some of us might be uncomfortable sleeping in the barrack where the explosion had occurred. So, on our first night back, Colonel Whitelaw, the camp commander, came into 12 Platoon just before lights out. He made no speech or pep talk of any kind, but quietly prepared to stay the night. A bed was made ready for him at the head of the platoon near the front door, where a table usually stood. Just before lights out, the cadets in their bunks turned their heads toward the colonel's bunk as he put his head down and settled in. The lights went out and all went quiet. Other than in an empty barrack, I had never heard it so still before. I think the boys were somewhat comforted by the colonel's presence. It was a kind gesture. He was gone, however, before they woke in the morning.

Investigation

"Sergeant Fostaty, you are wanted at The Bridge for the investigation," growled Sergeant Gutta at me down the orderly room hallway.

He was standing at the counter by the swinging gate holding a sheaf of papers, and caught me on my way through the common area and into 10 Platoon. I stopped in my tracks. I knew there would be more information on the heels of his first statement. Sergeant Gutta always threw out a statement that got your attention, and then the details or qualification followed. He lobbed it at me as soon as I faced him.

"You'll report there this afternoon with Gibeault."

It wasn't much of a follow-up, but that was all he was giving me. I knew, of course, that an investigation was under way—quite a few people already had been called to give evidence or answer questions. Every day for a week and a half after the explosion, people would disappear from training and reappear a few hours later. When they returned they were conspicuously silent about what had gone on during their questioning. We were in the last week of the camp, and I was one of the last to be called. I had never been called to any type of inquest before, and I was a bit excited.

"Yes, sir," was all that Sergeant Gutta expected of me right then, so I delivered it and thought I would seek out Bob Gibeault to fill me in on any details. The sergeant turned and disappeared into the orderly room, leaving me to digest the instruction.

I couldn't find Bob anywhere, so after lunch I thought I would park myself in the OR and wait for him to find me while the rest of the company went about the business of the afternoon's training.

I was leaning on the counter, enjoying the quiet and the few minutes of solitude and gazing through the open doorway when, in the distance, I saw Bob walking toward the company, his steps creating small clouds of dust as he strode on the sandy path. He walked up the steps through the main door and saluted—we generally entered the company through our respective platoons, but walking through the OR entrance obliged one to salute the officer on duty.

"It's just me here," I said.

"Force of habit," he replied with a smile.

He told me he had been at the inquiry that morning and evidently had returned too late to eat with the company. That explained why I couldn't find him earlier.

"When do we leave?" I asked.

"They'll have us picked up in a car when they are ready for us," he said.

"So, what do they want to know?" I inquired, smiling.

"I am not allowed to say," was his apologetic response.

•

Early in the afternoon, a black staff car sent up a cloud of dust as it made the tight turn in the sand and came to a stop at the door of the OR. The driver didn't get out of the car but sat there waiting for us. I let the dust settle before I approached and got into the back seat. As soon as I slammed the door, I cranked down the window to allow some breeze in. The sun was shining and the car was hot. Bob sat up front with the driver, and we were on our way to The Bridge. No one spoke. The wind rushing in the open windows was the only sound. I turned around and looked out the back window to see the trail we left. The dust lifted in our wake, obliterating what we were leaving behind.

We shot past the mess and snaked our way up the hill to the main part of the base where the roads were paved. There, we took the main road past the theatre, past building #502, out to the far side of the base, where we turned left down a small dirt road. I soon noticed signs marked "Restricted Area" and "No Entry." Small scrubby trees and brush lined both sides of the road, which looked as though it came to a dead end at a small circle where vehicles could turn around. As we got closer to the end of the road, however, I saw what looked at first like a hillock about the size of a very small house. Then I realized it was man-made, perfectly rounded, like an upside-down bowl, and sparsely covered with grass. At the side of the hill, there was a door.

The car pulled up to the front of the hill and Bob and I bailed out. He was heading for the hillock before I had even closed my car door. I followed, mystified. As we approached the door, our car swung around and drove off down the dirt road, raising another cape of dust behind it.

The air was hot and oppressive, and I could hear a cicada's electric whining in the distance and then another in reply. The cicadas stopped abruptly, leaving only the sound of Bob's boots crunching on the dirt path. Bob stopped at the door, and all was silent for a few seconds before I in turn began to walk toward the door, my boots crunching on the gravel where Bob's had moments before.

The hillock door looked like a windowed storm door on the front of a cottage. It was a bit old and weathered and needed some paint. A strange and very small place to hold an investigation, I thought. Through the door, it appeared dark and empty. Despite its name, this place also didn't look anything like a bridge. Bob reached for the door handle, and as he turned it, an alarm buzzer shattered the silence and made me jump. He and I stepped in quickly, and the buzzer stopped when the rickety door clicked shut behind us.

As my eyes began to adjust to the dim light inside, I saw that we were facing two huge metal double doors that hung from ceiling to floor. We took a few steps in, and Bob reached over to push a button on the wall by the door. A slit of a metal window slid open, and a pair of eyes flicked back and forth from Bob's face to mine. The window shut with a clink. Then a large metallic click was followed by the sound of a motor softly whirring. The doors opened to reveal a short, grey-green hallway. Our footsteps echoed as we walked toward another set of metal doors that were already beginning to open as the big metal doors slowly swung closed behind us. It was cooler here than it was outside.

Beyond the second set of doors, on the left-hand side, was a small office, consisting mostly of windows, almost like a toll booth. There, we signed in and received visitors' badges, and a guard gestured with an open hand to a set of stairs on the right. We descended numerous flights of stairs before reaching the bottom, where I followed Bob in turning right and walking down a long corridor lined with dark, solid-looking polished wooden doors with gold lettering. The labels on the closed doors read "Prime Minister," "Lt. Governor," "Premier," and various ministerial titles.

I didn't realize it at the time, but we must have been in one of the famous "Diefenbunkers"—nuclear fallout shelters secretly built in the early 1960s by the government of John Diefenbaker. Once there were seven, scattered across the country, but only three still exist. One is a museum near Ottawa and two are still under government control: one at CFB Borden, about one hundred kilometres north of Toronto, and the one in Valcartier, northwest of Quebec City, where Bob and I walked underground together that day.

The long hallway with the wooden doors emptied into a large room that held many shiny grey institutional metal desks and chairs. The desks all faced the same direction and were perfectly lined up. The chairs behind the desks were all placed exactly the same distance from the desks they served, and the desks had nothing on them. Beside every desk, in exactly the same spot, stood a garbage can that was empty and looked as though it had never been used. Even the seams of the metal garbage cans all faced the same direction. No fewer than twelve doors opened off to what I assumed must be small satellite offices. Most of the doors were closed, and their frosted glass windows revealed nothing beyond, except that the lights in all but two of the offices were off.

Other than Bob and me, only one other person was in the large central room, a private from the Royal 22nd Regiment. When we arrived, he was sitting, his chair leaning against the wall teetering on the two back legs. We must have surprised him, though, because he quickly rocked upright, slamming the front chair legs on the floor, as we entered. Bob leaned over and quietly told me the private was there to watch us. The private smiled at us wanly but didn't speak, and rocked back to his original perch. We obviously had not impressed him enough for him to feel he needed to mind his posture.

Bob led me to one of the small satellite offices where the door was open and the light was on. Out of the private's view, we sat down on austere metal chairs, which groaned on the linoleum-tiled floor as we moved them. I looked over at Bob, but he kept his gaze fixed at the wall and said nothing. My excitement began to curdle to anxiety. I suddenly became aware that the seriousness of the inquiry had made it necessary to bring me two storeys underground and encased in metres of concrete to answer a few questions. This wasn't an office in the basement of some office building. This was a nuclear fallout shelter.

I confess I knew a little of what to expect, which contributed to my growing unease. Some of the cadets in my platoon had been here before me, and one had let me know a little of what went on; strangely, though, no one had mentioned this sinister-feeling location. George Mawko had come back from the inquiry late one night, and when I asked him if he'd been at the inquiry all that time, his face twisted into a grimace, and he lowered his head to mask the fact that he was fighting tears.

"You mean the interrogation, Sergeant?" He whispered with agitation. "Yes, I was there tonight."

Mawko was an intelligent boy and not one to cry over a trifle. He was visibly shaken, so I wanted to know what had upset him. Still, I didn't want him to wake the others, so I gestured that we go out to the common area beside the NCOs' quarters. Once there, he wiped his eyes on his rolled-up sleeve, collected himself, and began to tell me about his experience at the inquiry.

"They tried to blame it on me!" he said, incredulously. "They made me tell the story, the whole story, over and over again." He stopped himself abruptly, and I could see he was again fighting tears. He said they had fired questions at him so quickly that they overlapped and he had trouble thinking straight. Eventually he calmed down again, but looked exhausted. I told him to go to bed. I would have let him sleep in a bit the next day, but a barrack in the morning is a noisy place, and he was soon up with the others.

I was jolted back to the present in the Diefenbunker when I heard the private's chair in the large outer office suddenly thump, and a captain appeared in the doorway to the small room where Bob and I waited. The captain looked around, and without so much as a preamble, demanded, "Where is Borgia?" We tried respectfully to stand up, but the captain dismissively hand signalled us to stay seated.

"He is on his way, sir," said Bob. "He had to eat lunch." Gaétan Borgia was a cadet in Bob's platoon. I had heard his name before, but I wasn't familiar with him. I guessed silently that he was the reason the car that had deposited us had left so quickly—it must have gone back to pick him up.

"Very well," said the captain. "Sergeant Gibeault, come with me, please."

Bob's chair groaned on the floor as he stood to follow, and the two disappeared from view. I sat there for a long time, not knowing what to do. There was nothing to look at but a map of Canada on the wall. From my seat, though, it was too far away for me to read the small print on it. I didn't dare stand up, in case I made a noise that would arouse the interest of the private, who somehow made me feel as though he was suspicious of something. In any case, in the silence of the bunker, it was terribly conspicuous whenever a chair moved. They were made of hollow tubular steel that resonated like an echo chamber, amplifying even the smallest movement.

Then in walked Borgia. He was tall and very fair, with freckles, and a shock of wavy, bright red hair. He sat down on the other side of the room and stared at the wall. Whether he was intimidated by me, or just shy, or had been told not to communicate with anyone, he never made eye contact with me while we waited together in that room.

After about forty-five minutes, Bob came back. He walked right by Borgia and me without so much as glancing at us and settled down in the small office next door. Five minutes later, the captain reappeared and said only, "Borgia." Borgia stood, accompanied by a loud groaning fanfare from his chair, and followed the captain out of sight.

Another three-quarters of an hour or so passed. It seemed endless. I couldn't see Bob—I assumed he'd been sent into the other office to keep us from communicating. I was going half out of my mind with anticipation and boredom when the captain came back and said, "Sergeant Fostaty." He turned and headed in the opposite direction, so I stood up, trying to keep the chair from announcing my departure. I followed him across the main room, where the private watched us go by as he poured himself a cup of coffee from the nearby machine.

The captain opened a door at the end of a hallway to reveal a space the size of a classroom. As I followed him inside, I turned my head to the right to see, in the centre of the room, five men: two lieutenant-colonels and three majors behind a long table. The room wasn't terribly bright, but the light was adequate over the table to see the gold bars on the epaulettes of their shirts. About three metres away and directly in front of the table, facing the panel of officers, was a single metal chair. Turning my head the other way, I saw, just beside the door on my left, a cardboard box with what I took to be an assortment of dummy rockets and explosives. The lieutenant-colonel in the centre of the group motioned for me to come in, so I walked to the centre of the room and came to attention beside the single chair, facing the officers. I heard the captain close the door behind me. An MP came forward and stood at my back.

"Salute!" he whispered sharply. I did. "Sit down," he said, and I heard him take a step back from me. I sat, and in silence the panel of officers looked me over and then at their notes.

At a smaller table just on my left, another man sat perpendicular to the examining officers, so he faced my left side. On the table in front of him was a small machine, an electronic device about thirty centimetres square and ten centimetres high. Attached to it was a plastic hose like the kind on old-fashioned hair dryers, surrounded by a spring that coiled from one end to the other. In his hand was what looked like a long cone or an oxygen mask. I was watching him put the mask up to his face when the colonel at the centre of the table said, "State your name, rank, and number."

"Fostaty, G.S. Sergeant," I said, followed by my number.

There was a tiny click, and the man with the oxygen mask began to repeat what I said. His voice was muffled as he spoke into the cone. I was surprised to hear my answer repeated. I felt like a child being mocked by a sibling. I wanted to look at him, but I thought that would be unacceptable. The next question brought me out of my amazement.

"What is your position?"

"Second in command of 10 Platoon, D Company."

Click. Again the man with the mask repeated what I'd said, word for word, as he had for the colonel's questions. At first, I found myself distracted by the repetition of the questions and answers. I was afraid I wouldn't hear the next question correctly if I was listening to my answers being repeated. But listening to my responses again gave me a chance to validate what I was saying.

The questions, though, began to come more quickly, and at times more than one person was questioning me at once, so that a new question would begin before I finished answering the previous one. There were fewer clicks as the questions came more frequently. I supposed the man with the oxygen mask didn't have time to stop and start the machine between questions; he just kept it rolling. I wondered why they didn't just record the proceedings as they occurred or use a stenographer, as in the movies, instead of having a third person repeat everything. I was not given time to linger over these speculations, though.

"Sergeant Fostaty, why did you come to the camp this summer?"

It was an unusual question, I thought. All the NCOs trained for a number of years as cadets in the hope that we would be promoted and invited to participate.

"I've taken cadet training for five years, and I have qualified to be an NCO, Sir, so therefore I came this summer." As soon as it left my mouth, I thought, Is that the best I could come up with?

"Do you have anything against anyone in your company?"

"No, Sir."

"Did you?"

"No, Sir." I didn't like where this was going.

"Do you collect souvenirs?"

"Yes, Sir."

"What kind of souvenirs?"

"Cap badges and flashes."

His eyes widened and then he asked, "What sort of flashes?"

"Shoulder flashes and, actually, all sorts of insignia."

"Oh." He seemed disappointed and made a note.

The colonel changed his direction: "What did you do when you heard the explosion?"

I explained everything, giving all the facts that I could remember, from the moment we met the injured Lieutenant Katzko in the hallway up to the point where all the injured cadets were taken to the hospital. And then I stopped. I heard my last statement echoed, and then the man with the oxygen mask stopped, too, after repeating my last words. The panel stared at me without a word. The looks on their faces seemed to say, go on, so I asked, "Shall I continue, Sir?"

"Yes," said the colonel. So I did, ending soon after I began again, where it seemed there was no more to tell. I heard my last bit of information echoed by the man with the oxygen mask. There were some moments of silence again, as they made a few notes. One by one they finished their note taking and looked up at me. I thought I might be finished. I was wrong.

They started firing questions at me, literally, from left and right. I would no sooner finish answering a question from the officer at one end of the table than the officer at the other end would sharply ask another, causing me to look from side to side as though watching a tennis match. If my answer was not going in the direction they wanted, they would just cut me off with another question. It was a miracle that the man with the oxygen mask could keep up with them.

"Did you know your cadets well?"

"Yes."

"How well?"

"I know them well enough to know how they will react to an order or request just by the expression on their fac…"

"What about Mawko?"

"What about him, Sir?" I couldn't see why they would want to single out Mawko.

"What is he like?"

"He is a very intelligent boy, Sir."

"How do you know?"

"By the way he speaks, acts, and conducts himself…"

"Is he a troublemaker?"

"No, Sir."

They kept going and I kept answering, while the man with the oxygen mask kept clicking and repeating everything. Then they started repeating questions I had already answered. I noticed a decided change in their tone, too. They seemed to be challenging what I said, even things that were obvious or self-evident. They would ask a question and then one would make a face, or another might roll his eyes at one of my answers. I started to become very uncomfortable with the way I was being questioned, and I started to second-guess my own answers. The way they were questioning me was both accusatory and dismissive.

At times, two people at once would ask different questions. I would try to answer both, looking at the officer who asked while I answered, and then quickly turning to look at the other questioning officer to answer his question, before still another question interrupted me. I have no idea how the man in the oxygen mask dealt with that; I had my hands too full to listen to him. I felt like I was being interrogated, like they were looking to have someone take responsibility for even the smallest thing that went wrong, so that the whole house of cards would fall at his feet…my feet.

"What was Lloyd like?…Who were the troublemakers of the platoon?…Would Vallée lie to save his own ass?…Scratch ass. Put in skin," he said, turning toward the man with the oxygen mask, who nodded. Continuing with me, "Would Vallée lie to save his own skin?"

Then they slowed down.

"Let's talk about Adventure Training," said the colonel at the centre of the table, who was obviously in charge. There was a pause.

In Adventure Training, the cadets were taken out into the bush to live under improvised shelters made with our ponchos for a few days. They were taught to construct a bivouac, they learned survival techniques such as moving around in the bush, staying warm and dry, hygiene, safety, and finding food as well as outdoor cooking, orienteering, bridge building, and how to leave as little impact as possible on the environment. It was all a part of the leadership training, where they had to learn to rely on each other for everything and work together to accomplish their tasks and meet their objectives.

"Did you have a kit inspection after the Adventure Training?" asked the colonel.

"Yes, Sir."

"Where did you search?"

"In barrack boxes, in pockets, under jackets, between blankets, under pillows, under sheets, under beds, on the rafters, in the washrooms, in the fire extinguishers, under the barracks, inside boots…"

"Stop."

"Sir?"

"Why under the barracks?" The whole panel looked up at me.

"Because, that is where we hid things when we were cadets."

"Like what?"

"*Playboy* magazines, beer…"

"At Adventure Training, would a cadet have a chance to get away from the rest of the platoon?"

"Not likely, Sir."

"Why?" he said, as if he didn't believe me.

"Because I conducted a head count every ten to fifteen minutes, and my corporals did the same, so, if you figure it out, there was a head count, on average, every five or six minutes."

"Very thorough. You and your corporals are very good NCOs," he said as he folded his hands in front of him on the table.

"Thank you, Sir."

"Would one or two be able to leave for a legitimate reason?"

"Like, to use the toilet, Sir?"

"Yes."

"Yes, Sir." He made a note.

"Well, Sergeant Fostaty, how do you class yourself as an NCO?"

"I don't know, Sir. I am not in a position to judge myself. I would hope that I am a good NCO." This answer sounded lame even to me. I was sure this marked me as a complete fool to them.

"What is your position in your cadet corps?"

"I am a captain, training officer, and instructor, Sir."

"What do you instruct?"

"Rope Bridging, Radio Communications, and Search and Rescue, Sir."

He paused for a moment, looking me in the eyes before saying, "You seem to be an intelligent young man, Sergeant." He paused again. I didn't think he wanted me to reply to that; it seemed to be a preamble for an additional question. I was right. "Have you ever seen a live grenade?" he asked.

"Only smoke and white-phosphorous, Sir." I was thinking about some training and demonstration I had had at Camp Farnham a few years before.

He unclasped his hands and reached down to the floor beside his left leg and brought a small canister up to the table. It was a cylinder about the size of a soup can, only it was made not of tin but something like cardboard and coloured olive green. He twisted the cylinder apart and slid out an M-61 grenade.

"This is a live grenade," he said with his eyebrows raised and what I thought was the slightest hint of a smile. The colonel held the live grenade up by the bottom, perched on his fingertips, while resting his elbow on the table. Putting his elbow on the table necessitated him to lean forward. The effect was as if he was admiring a delicate peach. The grenade was dark green and smooth. I remember seeing the striker lever and the safety pin with its ring still there, in place. I knew enough about grenades to know it was armed and ready for use.

Meanwhile the man in the oxygen mask clicked and repeated, "This is a live grenade."

"What the hell are you doing with that in here?" I said, before thinking. It came out of me like a breathy gasp. They pretended not to hear, and the man with the oxygen mask did not repeat it. The colonel carefully, and ceremoniously, lifted his elbow off the table and slid the grenade back into the cylinder, replaced the top, and set it down gently on the table in front of him.

"You may leave now," he said abruptly and dismissively. Then he turned his attention to his notes. He was through with me.

My knees were trembling as I stood to attention and saluted without any prompting from the MP, who was still standing behind me. It was a good salute: crisp and sharp and perfect. Canadian military etiquette did not allow capless officers to salute in return, but I wanted to be acknowledged—I wanted that tiny bit of respect back. The colonel at the centre was still making notes and looking down at his papers. The other officers were looking at me and glancing over at him. I could have left it at that, but I held my salute until he finally looked up and gave me the slightest nod to acknowledge it.

"Good day, Sir," I said, then did an about-turn and headed for the door. I wanted to do this by the book. The MP opened the door for me to leave and shut it behind me. I stopped and exhaled.

I didn't get a chance to sit down again. As I weakly approached the small waiting room, Bob and Borgia saw me coming and stood up. We made our way out through the hallway with the dark wooden monogrammed doors, back up to ground level, through all the security doors, and out to the front, where the staff car was idling, waiting to take us back.

After the cool air underground, the hot, still air outside was a bit of a shock. We were silent on the way back to the company. My whole body felt heavy as I sat in the back seat beside Borgia. I had the window down again so that the noise of the wind would discourage anyone from speaking to me. I turned my head to face the outside, but I don't remember the trip back. I was replaying the afternoon in my head so that I wouldn't forget. Days later, although no one went into any detail about the questions and answers, a few of us joked and laughed about the inquiry. It was an uneasy laughter.

Summer 1974 Closes

In the last week of our stay at CFB Valcartier, we received notice that our platoon photos were ready for pickup. Some were of the whole platoon gathered together, others were candid shots. Occasionally throughout the days of training, and at leisure time, too, we would hear the click of a camera shutter and catch a camp photographer lowering his camera and moving on to his next unsuspecting subjects. I knew from years before that some really great pictures had been taken and I had kicked myself for not ordering any.

So this summer, before the explosion, I had squinted at contact sheets of tiny pictures, trying to determine if a microscopic figure was me or not. With everyone virtually dressed the same and all the photos in black and white, it was not an easy task. Eventually, I got my turn with a loupe to have a magnified look at the figures in the picture. There wasn't much time to scrutinize composition, lighting, or if they caught me at my best. A lineup of people behind me were already grumbling, so I ordered three photos I could find with me in them.

When we heard they were ready, I went at the first opportunity to the photo studio, at the end of the administration complex right beside the barber shop. I had to wait in a long line to get inside to pay and pick up my envelope. Then I hurried back outside and pulled out the photos on my way back to my quarters. The first was a great picture of three smiling friends: me with Banzal and Bruce. There must have

been a break in the firing relay on the rifle range, and we had struck
a pose together, ear protection in hand.

The outdoor range, where the cadets received training in shooting,
had sixteen firing positions spaced a few metres apart. The cadets
would be brought over in a row of sixteen or fewer, each to stand
behind a firing position. On command they would step forward and
lie prone on a poncho beside a rifle. Ammunition in a magazine would
be brought and placed beside the rifle and, again on command, the
cadet would load the magazine in the rifle. About ninety metres away,
targets were raised, and the range officer would give the order to load
and fire. After each relay, the targets would be lowered for the scores
to be recorded. Four or five NCOs would stand behind the cadets on
the firing line to monitor activity and keep everything safe while the
range officer called out the commands. Our job was to ensure that the
rifles were always pointed down range, watch for misfires, and help
anyone having difficulty.

I flipped to the third photo in my hands and saw another one
from the range. In this one, I am giving direction to a cadet on the
firing line. The photographer must have called out to us because we
are both looking a bit surprised in the direction of the lens. Then I
stopped walking and shuddered: the cadet in the foreground was Mario
Provencher from 11 Platoon, one of the boys who was killed. I slowly
pushed it beneath the other pictures and slid it back into the envelope.
I walked back to my quarters feeling anxious, guilty, and stupid.

Also that last week of the camp, a few NCOs went to visit some of
our cadets who were still in hospital—the ones they would let us see.
We never did get to see those who'd been seriously injured. We did see
Lieutenant Katzko, though. His belly wound was more serious than they
had first suspected. We were told that he had sustained liver damage.
He seemed genuinely pleased to see us when we arrived. He said he
was feeling all right, and he was smiling, but he was pale and his hair
was unkempt. It was strange to see him out of uniform, lying in bed
in a pastel-coloured hospital gown. We asked him about the nurses,
of course, and naturally he complained about the food. We were soon

(From left to right) Fostaty, Banzal, and Bruce.

chivvied away by a nurse—there were too many of us in the room and we were being overly cheerful. We all wished him well and split up to visit the cadets from our own platoons before the visiting hour was over. That was the last time I saw Katzko; we didn't return to the hospital, and he went on medical leave, I was told.

We also never pursued the matter of sending Botosan home. It seemed like a much too trivial matter after all that had happened, and he seemed to have mellowed, too, becoming almost invisible. I had only

Cadets in training on the firing line at the rifle range; Mario Provencher is front and centre.

one disagreement with him after July 30, and it was relatively minor. During the rehearsals for the memorial parade to honour the boys who had died, Botosan was chosen to be the Right Marker, who is called out to the parade square to stand on a prearranged mark. Each group, whether a section, platoon, or company, has its own Right Marker, with whom it aligns when called onto the parade square.

When taking his place as the Right Marker for our company, though, Botosan's gait was noticeably slower and his paces longer than those of the Markers from the other companies, making him appear conspicuously out of step with all the other Markers, as they headed for different locations on the parade square. When I questioned him about the discrepancy, he argued that his was the regulation 110 paces per minute for Highland regiments, of which he was a member, and that he would not change. I let him know that he was currently training with an armoured regiment, le 12ᵉ Régiment blindé, and that its cadence was the standard 120 paces per minute.

"I am a Highlander," was his response.

"So you are," I said.

I wasn't going to make a bigger issue of it. It didn't seem worth the trouble, and if it did cause a problem for the battalion as a whole, I was sure the RSM would be the first one to speak with him. I would like to have seen him nose to nose with the RSM; however, the next time the Markers were called out in the rehearsal, Botosan marched out to his spot, to my surprise, in step with the others. I guess all he needed was to have a small victory to be appeased.

Everyone else seemed to forget about sending Botosan home as well. It was my report that would have put him on the bus, but I never went back to finish it. At first, we were quartered at the chapel, not at the company, so I couldn't get to it, and there were too many other things to attend to anyway. Later, when we moved back into the barracks, I forgot about it for a time because he had begun to behave himself, leaving us to worry and talk about other things. Finally, I realized, too, that had he not acted the way he did, I would have never had the occasion to initiate the report, and instead of sitting hunched over a

The memorial parade in 1974 at CFB Valcartier.

typewriter in the orderly room hunting and pecking with two fingers, I would most certainly have been in the barrack when the grenade went off. His poor behaviour had kept me from being injured, or worse. This was pure serendipity. I didn't express my gratitude by telling him I wouldn't pursue his expulsion, though; I simply let it go.

The memorial parade was held about ten days after the explosion. The whole battalion was on parade in front of building #502. A reviewing stand had been built for the occasion at the front of the parade square, and seven torches had been lit for seven who had died there that summer: six were for D Company members and one for

Claude Charbonneau. Sergeant Gutta read the Twenty-third Psalm
and our company commander, Major Brochu, called their names. The
response to each name was a single bell chime and the extinguishing of
one of the torches. We were placed in the second row of companies, so
I couldn't see the torches or the dais from where Major Brochu called
out the names, but it was the first time we heard officially who had
died that day: Yves Langlois, Pierre Leroux, Eric Lloyd, Othon Mangos,
Mario Provencher, and Michel Voisard. Then, Paul Wheeler and Mark
Slater were given certificates of commendation for their efforts on the
day of the explosion. Paul looked a bit uncomfortable when people
asked to see the certificate later that day.

The very short ceremony came too soon after the event for me
to understand or appreciate the impact it had, and would continue
to have, on me. No one had asked any of us how we were doing or
if we needed to talk about what had happened. We wouldn't have
asked for help ourselves. We were too young and filled with bravado to
understand that we, also, were victims. Our injuries were subtle and the
damage was hidden below a veneer highly polished by testosterone and
bluster. The realization that we, too, were hurt was not evident then,
but would take years to surface. We were never reassured that we had
done a good job or the right things. Neither were we debriefed on the
incident. I thought then that it was because I hadn't done my job well
or I hadn't done enough, that I had failed in my responsibility to my
cadets. I would learn much later that I wasn't alone in feeling this way.
That guilt and pain would cripple friendships and marriages, sabotage
sleep, and wreak untold damage as it lay dormant for years.

During those last few days on the base between August 11 and 18,
some recruiters informally approached me and some of the others to
make a commitment to continue with the regular forces. There were
attractive salary promises and assurances of rank and rapid promotion.
I was dogged by a feeling of failure, though. I was demoralized. Because
no one remarked on what we had gone through, either to critique or
to commend, I took my superiors' silence as an indictment. I felt I was

an embarrassment, a disappointment much better to be ignored. I had had enough for now. It was time to move on.

Moving on was not straightforward. We were not invited to any of the funerals for our fellow cadets; in fact, we didn't hear a thing about them. At the memorial on the base, we had paid honour to the dead briefly, but no one ever mentioned those of us left behind. No one ever recalled those who had dragged their friends to safety, put dressings on ghastly wounds, and carried stretchers to ambulances. Brave people had run back into the barrack time and again without knowing what had caused the explosion or whether another might happen at any second. They were young, but exceptional, those who had watched their friends die, identified their bodies, and then been expected to return to business as usual. They did so, and without complaint, and they were immediately and conveniently forgotten.

I held the childish hope that, eventually, someone would rescue me from that day. I waited for the longest time, but rescue never came. I think the administrative officers at the base were expecting, or hoping, that someone else would take care of it, while the officers at our home units didn't understand what we had gone through. Our families didn't know either, mistakenly thinking that what had happened, had happened *near* us not *to* us. We dispersed throughout the province soon afterward, and we had been conditioned to accept that what had happened was not important, so we believed our residual feelings were abnormal and no one talked about it.

Just before the end of our term at the base, we decided to give Sergeant Gutta a parting gift. He had already done so much for us and had made such an impact on us that we wanted to show our appreciation in a way that would be meaningful, yet not frivolous. A gag gift or a card would not have done. We needed something practical and long-lasting that would be appropriate for his character. We settled on a watch. We fourteen NCOs pooled our money, and a couple of the guys went to the city on their next leave to purchase one. They came back with the perfect watch: rugged, elegant, and practical looking.

We presented our gift to him one morning in the OR before the training day began. He was completely taken aback, although he certainly didn't bluster or gush, or even smile. His silence was the most telling of all as he just stared at the watch in the open box. Then, after the longest pause, he looked up and simply, seriously, and quite quietly, said, "Thank you. Merci." I could see he was moved by the gesture.

Early the next day, while we were getting organized for the movement of people to their lectures, I bumped into him in the OR and noticed he was wearing the watch. I thought I would be clever and, with a smile, I said, "Nice watch! Where'd you get it?"

He turned to me, his face like stone. I stopped in my tracks as I felt the blood go to my face. I knew I had said the wrong thing as soon as it had left my mouth. Now, I was waiting for the hammer to fall. He waited a few seconds as the last of the others bustled out of the room.

"Don't be a smart ass," he snapped, and held my gaze while I dissolved with discomfort and shame.

"Yes, Sir. I am sorry, Sir."

I was never so embarrassed in my life. I had acted like a fool in front of the person I most respected in the world. He could have reprimanded me in front of the other NCOs, but he had waited until they'd left. He had shown me respect even when I had crossed the boundary of respectful behaviour toward him.

"Very well," he said. "We'll say no more about it"; and, with a nod, I was dismissed.

He never mentioned it again, and as far as I could tell, he never treated me any differently than the others. I never forgot those short few seconds of humiliation, the lesson I learned, and how someone could wield power with grace and finesse.

●

In mid-August, buses arrived throughout the last day of camp to take the cadets in groups to their hometowns in different parts of the province. I watched my brother leave early, his brown duffel bag balanced high up on his shoulder. He would be home by suppertime. He didn't wave or say goodbye. We knew we would see each other soon. The company was gradually emptying out. By the middle of the afternoon, all the cadets would be gone and we NCOs would be finished our work. There would be nothing left to do but turn in our gear and head back to our homes and home units.

I remember going to the mess and standing in the long line for our last pay parade. I was there alone from D Company in that crowd of NCOs from the whole camp. The others either had come already or would come later. For some reason, I had made the trip to the mess alone. I slowly moved forward as each person was carefully checked off the list and his cash counted out. I finally came to the head of the line and saluted. The paymaster, a captain, was seated at a table with cases of money at his side, stacks of money on the table, and flanked by two MPs, one with a machine gun and one with a holstered sidearm. The captain wasn't wearing a cap, so he didn't salute back; he didn't even acknowledge my salute. He looked bored, having done this hundreds of times already today, and he would continue until we were all paid. The line behind me stretched through the centre of the mess and back to the door, so he would be here for some time yet.

As I stated my name and number, chatter and laughter broke out far behind me where some newcomers were just joining the line. The paymaster looked up from his list and with an annoyed expression, thrust his chin in the general direction of the disturbance. One of the MPs quickly barked "Silence!" The mess instantly went quiet. Some hushed laughter rippled at the back of the line. The MP lifted his hand and pointed a threatening finger at the offender at the back of the mess, silencing him. There was no talking allowed in the pay parade line. The paymaster returned his attention to me, arching his eyebrows to get my name and number again, which I repeated. He scanned the list with his finger and found my name. He then counted my final pay.

The mess was so quiet that I could hear the fip-fip-fip of the twenties as he counted them, and then the hiss of the bills on the table as he pushed them toward me. I signed for my pay and thought, This is the last time. The paymaster, not realizing that this was a turning point in my life, barely glanced at me as I saluted again and left. I slowly walked back to my quarters, looking around at the camp for the last time while still in uniform. The place seemed deserted.

I took the shortcut back to the company, the same route I had taken back from the mess every day; the way Paul and I had gone when we bumped into the second lieutenants every morning; the way I ran back from the medical inspection room on the day of the explosion when I feared I had lost Nick; and the path I had followed when I looked at the pictures and found Mario staring back at me. It was all over, I thought.

I also had a last look at the empty barrack alone that day. With the cadets gone, the sound of the camp was completely different—no rippling of chatter or shuffling of movement, no shouts of commands in the distance, only the sound of the late August breeze in the clutch of trees outside. Technically, this was no longer 12 Platoon barrack, but building #CC3-E. Next year they might designate it as another of the three numbers for this company: 10, 11, or 12. (When I was a cadet here, the same building had been called 10 Platoon.) I walked through it now, slowly, so as not to disturb the somehow unsettling quiet.

Trauma aside, the cadets had been changed this summer. They were now leaders. Their training had taught them to work together as a team and to appreciate the roles others took in their lives. Perhaps they now understood that many small flames can create a bright light, and that even the smallest flame makes a valuable contribution. They would now take that training home to their home units and pass some of it along. Although they wouldn't notice it themselves, their parents would notice that they now walked a little straighter and stood a little taller.

I looked down the row of bunks to appreciate that they had all been prepared true evacuation-style, with the thin mattresses rolled up on the foot of the beds, exposing the springs. The bedding was on top of the mattresses, placed blanket, blanket, sheet, sheet, pillowcase, and pillow on the top to make it easy for the support company to collect them for cleaning and then storage. The empty barrack boxes were on the beds, too, at the head of the bed on the bare springs. I stood still for a few moments, listening to my own breathing and drinking in the silence. There was no hint of the tragedy that had happened here three weeks ago. It was rebuilt, painted, and polished, and all for $1,181.71 — the total bill for the repair of the barrack.[43] The cost would be paid for years.

There were murmurs, too, that the deceased cadets' families had been compensated for the loss of their sons. Large sums of money were hinted at, although no one volunteered any details. I didn't know where the information came from, but I had no reason to disbelieve it—compensation could explain the complete silence afterward and the absence of any news of subsequent litigation.

I mistakenly thought the event would hang over the base like a pall, and that no one would ever want to be a member of D Company again. The next group, though, would have no idea of it. At most, there would be some rumour or whisper, but the incident had started to become veiled in the three weeks that had passed since it occurred. By next summer, it would be buried and forgotten.

I left 12 Platoon barrack and walked into my own 10 Platoon. I wanted to call my platoon to attention one last time, but they were long gone. To them, I was already forgotten. When they left, they took my stripes, and a part of my identity, with them. I went to bed that night preoccupied with thoughts of getting back home again, of getting back to what was normal. I took comfort in the belief I would put the summer of 1974 behind me, and I would not dwell on it.

When I opened my eyes the next morning, I automatically brought my arm up to see my watch. It was only 0430. I wouldn't have to catch the bus home for a few hours yet, so I tried to get some more sleep. I didn't realize then that, although I was going home, I would not leave Valcartier—the memories would stay with me for the rest of my life.

Archival Discoveries

Decades later, combing through the information I had received from DND through the *Access to Information Act*, I had a much clearer idea of what had gone on beyond my sight at the base in 1974. But I still didn't know what news people outside the base had received from the press in 1974.

My need to know the full story prodded me on. I thought I would look through newspapers archives, and was surprised to find as little as I did. We are spoiled now by this information age in which we live. The current news media and the outlets that masquerade as news organizations seem to be able to grind out massive volumes of information based on little data, but the only whiff of reporting I saw in the days just following the explosion was a headline in a Quebec tabloid that declared the incident a massacre.

I thought that perhaps newspapers outside Quebec had offered more coverage, but I was wrong. Most papers shared the same newswire services and ran identical stories. The *New York Times* noted it on August 1, 1974, and Harry Reasoner mentioned it on the *ABC News* on July 30, the day of the explosion. I have assembled here everything I could find thirty-four years after the fact: lean material for an event that made such an enduring impact on so many lives.

On Wednesday, July 31, 1974, the day after the explosion, the *Toronto Star* had the incident on the front page with a continuation on page sixteen.[44] Our story had shared the page with John Ehrlichman's conviction for his involvement in the Watergate scandal, Richard

Nixon's impeachment proceedings, and the opening of the Toronto Zoo, which featured a photo of an orangutan that was four times the size of the article on the explosion at Valcartier.

The paper printed the names of the cadets who had died; other than that, the amount of incorrect information was startling. The number of people injured was wrong, the paper reporting 32 instead of the actual 54. The number of people in the barrack at the time of the explosion was also wrong — 60 to 75 people rather than the 138 who had been there. A witness had reported it took seven minutes to get the first victim to the hospital. I had knelt beside that first ambulance. It would have been impossible to drive to the hospital in only seven minutes. I would like to know who that witness was, too. None of us could have spoken to the press — the base had been locked down, and no one could get either in or out.

The thing that struck me the hardest was that the reporter must have collected his information, written the piece, and submitted it long before those of us at the scene knew what was going on. The *Toronto Star* would have been delivered the morning after the explosion. We didn't find out for days that six boys had been killed or any of the details about who was critically injured.

On Thursday, October 24, 1974, three months after the explosion, the *Toronto Star* reported on page nine that the grenade blast was still a mystery. The coroner told the inquest that he was dissatisfied: "The main point remains a mystery."[45] The paper did not report, however, what the main point was. Although the Military Police and the Sûreté du Québec had finished their investigations, a coroner's inquest was by then under way, presided over by coroner Armand Drouin, who was quoted as saying he would re-examine the testimony and have a decision in mid-December. It was not reported what the decision would be about.

Asked at the coroner's inquest if he could accidentally have taken a live grenade from the box, Captain Giroux, who had given the explosives safety lecture to the cadets, replied, "I would have known if it had been a live explosive."[46] He then commented that he had turned his back on the box for a moment to answer a question from a cadet shortly before the explosion. When asked if he could have circulated a green grenade among the cadets, he responded, "There is a possibility that an error could have been made."[47] It was an odd way to answer, I thought. By saying that an error could have been made, and not "I could have made an error," he seems to be trying to dissociate himself from the possibility that he was responsible.

On May 26, 2009, I received a newspaper clipping from Gary Katzko in an email. The scanned clipping arrived with the name of the newspaper missing; "Brain damaged cadet gets his stripes," announced the headline. It was yellowed and dated November 11, 1974—about three and a half months after the explosion. Yves Sénécal, a cadet from 11 Platoon who was injured in the explosion, had recently celebrated his fifteenth birthday in the hospital. Fifteen of his friends from his cadet corps visited him, bringing gifts, and he was awarded his sergeant's stripes in his hospital bed. Sénécal had lost his hearing, speech, and coordination. He could only smile. The article reported that the doctors didn't yet know the full extent of the damage to him.

The coroner's inquest found Captain Giroux criminally responsible for the grenade explosion: "Giroux, 30, neglected his duties as instructor by not checking of dummy grenades to ascertain there were no live grenades among them."[48] The coroner also chastised three of the captain's subordinates and criticized the higher base authorities. The *Toronto Star* of Wednesday, March 12, 1975, quoted him as saying, "I do not hesitate to blame the high authorities of the base for their apathy and disinterest which seemed to have led to a climate of negligence and thoughtlessness."[49] The *Star* article also reported that the coroner had further concluded the direct and immediate cause of the tragedy was that the captain did not check the dummies before the instruction began. A spokesman for the armed forces said they would consult with the Quebec justice minister to approve their proceeding with the matter in accordance with military law.[50]

About a month and a half after the coroner's finding, Giroux pleaded not guilty to the charge of criminal negligence. A preliminary hearing was set for August 19, 1975. A tiny article in the *Toronto Star* on Wednesday, April 23, 1975, entitled "Grenade case man denies charge" and buried under a highlighted article about an anti-pollution show, does not mention the location or whether it was to be a civil or military hearing.[51]

A communiqué from Military Police to National Defence Headquarters and the Judge Advocate General at CFB Valcartier states that the defence ended its case in the preliminary hearing for a civil trial and asked Judge Paul-Émile Fortin to bring the court on a visit to the munitions depot and the cadet camp at Valcartier on April 5, 1976, to help the judge form a better vision of the facts. This was granted.[52]

On June 21, 1977, the case in the civil trial was closed when Judge Anatole Corriveau of the Quebec Court of Sessions found Giroux not guilty of the charges against him.[53]

I began to see that the farther we moved away from the explosion on the calendar, the less space it took up in print, the deeper into the newspapers our story went, and the less important it became. It was almost comical that, on Friday May 21, 1976, the *Toronto Star* jammed a tiny, one-column, sixteen-line mention in between a public works tender and the obituaries. This column got the cadets' ages wrong, said they had been engaged in a weapons-handling class, and lowered the number of injured to thirteen. The article stated that Captain Giroux would have to stand trial on a charge of criminal negligence in the deaths of the six cadets. A trial date was not set.[54] The *Lethbridge Herald*, probably subscribing to the same newswire source, made the same errors in a May 12 story.[55]

Coverage came to an end in June 1977, almost three years after the explosion. On June 21, 1977, in the Quebec Court of Sessions, Giroux was found not guilty of the charges against him. The *Lethbridge Herald* quoted Judge Corriveau as saying that the captain had been a scapegoat for several negligent soldiers. The judge continued that, "when the testimony is contradictory, as in this case...we cannot consider that he did not care about the danger posed by a live grenade to the cadets in his class."[56] Testimony had shown negligence was evident somewhere, the judge said. The article further indicated that Giroux was "greatly relieved" by the verdict. He had been instructing at the base since the time of the accident, except for a short period spent recovering from his injuries. The conviction of criminal negligence would have carried a maximum penalty of life imprisonment.[57]

An unrelated picture to the left of the story in the *Lethbridge Herald* depicts a smiling fifteen-year-old boy holding up some golf-ball-sized hailstones that had fallen in a freak summer storm outside his house.[58] I couldn't help thinking that this was the sort of thing with which fifteen-year-olds should concern themselves.

Reunions

Thirty-four years after the explosion, with no contact all that time, I found myself in frequent touch with my former company sergeant major, Charles Gutta. He was attempting to bring as many of us together as possible for the next annual memorial parade, in July 2008. He had started the plans only a few months ago, but was now in touch with many of the old boys, as well as some NCOs, company officers, and our old cadet camp commander.

Gutta's years of retirement hadn't slowed him down. He had found most of us by searching the Internet and by boldly making inquiries. He was making most of the arrangements and delegating responsibilities to organize a reunion of sorts. I made the mistake of greeting him as "Sir" one day on the phone.

"It is Charles," he very quickly corrected me. "We are all the same, now."

"Of course, Charles." I said. He was still in charge.

•

My mobile phone buzzed on my hip as I stood on an Ottawa corner in the wind and rain of a March day, waiting for a cab. I have never become used to the feeling of a vibrating phone. It always takes me by surprise, like receiving an electrical shock. I was going to ignore the call and let it go to voicemail. I had come to Ottawa for the day on business, but my meeting was finished and I was trying to get to the airport in time to catch a flight home, which I figured I would now surely miss. The meeting had run long, so my colleagues had gone on ahead, leaving me to finish up and collect the presentation materials we had brought with us. So there I stood, trying to blink away rain that felt like bullets in my squinting eyes, with both hands full and my phone electrocuting my hip.

The phone kept buzzing. It wasn't going to voicemail as it usually did. I knew it had to be a colleague phoning to let me know something was amiss with my flight, or worse. In a panic, I clamped my briefcase and the projector tightly between my knees to free up my hands and get to the phone under my coat. I was trying to avoid getting the projector or my briefcase wet on the rain-soaked sidewalk. I turned my back into the wind, flipped up the hem of my jacket to get at the phone, and had just lifted it to my ear when a cab pulled up.

"Hold on a minute!" I yelled into the phone. I flung open the back door of the cab with my free pinky, threw the phone onto the back seat, and pulled the briefcase and projector in behind me. "The airport," I told the driver, as I slammed the door and began to look for the phone. I watched it skitter across the seat and then slide to the floor as the driver made a wild U-turn on Sussex Drive in front of the US Embassy and headed in the other direction.

"Hang on!" I reassured the caller, as I reached for the phone and finally brought it up to my ear. "Much better," I said. "So, what's going on?" I was hoping that the flight was delayed but not cancelled.

"Where are you?" the voice asked.

"On Sussex, in a cab, heading for the airport."

"In Ottawa?"

"Where else?" Wait a minute. This wasn't right. "Who is this?"

"It's Charles. What are you doing here in Ottawa?"

I switched gears and explained why I was here. The cabbie must have known I was in a hurry because he was exceeding every speed limit, weaving in and out as though pursued.

"What time's your flight?" Charles asked.

"Three o'clock."

"I'm on my way." He was going to the airport.

"Wait. I really won't have much time. I think I am just going to make the flight as it is." I was trying to sound as apologetic as I felt.

"You'll be fine. It's no trouble. I'll see you there." He hung up.

I had checked into my flight using my phone in the cab and I didn't have any luggage, so when I arrived at the airport, I quickly printed a boarding pass at the kiosk and headed straight toward security, scanning the interior of the building for anyone who could be Charles. We hadn't seen each other in thirty-four years, and I had no idea what to look for except a man about seventy who looked as though he were looking for someone. I was sure he, too, couldn't have picked me out of a lineup.

I had exhausted my hasty scan in the check-in area of the terminal as I breezed through. I was on my way to the escalator down to security clearance and the departure gates when my phone buzzed. It was a text from one of my colleagues: "Flight delayed 20 mins." I still had some time left.

I should have known Charles would have positioned himself at a choke point to find me. He would know that everyone had to go through security, and there he stood at the bottom of the escalator, watching me as I rode down behind a cluster of other people. His hair was snow white and his face stern as I looked at him looking at me. As I glided down the escalator toward the bottom, he began to smile. I took a few steps toward him and I was about to say, "Charles," when he pre-empted me with, "I knew it had to be you."

"I won't have much time, I'm afraid. Just a few minutes," I apologized.

He looked over at security. "There's no lineup. You'll get through in no time." He was right, naturally. "I'll keep an eye on the crowd, and if we see a wave coming down the escalator, I'll cut you loose." Still in charge.

It was good to shake his hand. It was strong and reassuring. He wasted no time. He wanted my help to locate as many of the others as we could. He brought out a sheet of paper to reference as we talked.

He had the names of a few people whom he wanted me to verify as having been with us in 1974. His plan was that, as we found someone, ideally he in turn would find one or two others. We spoke for a few minutes, and then I had to catch my flight. We shook hands again. He would be in touch.

One of my colleagues had seen my meeting with Charles from the other side of security.

"Who was that?" he asked.

"My old boss," I dodged.

"From where?"

"Oh, it's a long story and a long time ago," I said. I wasn't ready to tell the story yet. "They're boarding our flight," I said changing the subject. "Let's go."

•

Charles had inspired more activity with regard to a reunion. Small gatherings were planned in other cities where there were clusters of ex-D Company members, offers of help to organize, and one of my old 10 Platoon members set up a dedicated Web page with a message board where people could post notes and engage in discussions. It was a private page, only available to those who were verified as members of the company, in an effort to keep out the prying eyes of strangers, gawkers, and, believe it or not, pretenders. As people joined the site, email messages began to fly back and forth and old photos were scanned and posted there. We had started to come together.

I exchanged a few cautious messages with a few people. From some of the messages being traded, I could see there were differing levels of sensitivity and discretion. I enjoyed the nostalgia of connecting with a few people, but there seemed an undercurrent of discomfort in many of the messages, as though we were reaching out warily to one other. Admittedly, we had not spoken in many years, but the last time we were together we had been boys in uniform, not subject to the distractions of adult responsibilities such as relationships, children, work, and home life, and we weren't yet acquainted with grown-up diplomacy. Although some said they were looking forward to a reunion at the memorial service, others clearly were not interested. Others, too, were still hurting and bitter. The varying degrees of pain were as disparate as the people affected, and so were the ways the pain manifested within them.

I had a lucky chance to meet Aleth Bruce face to face. After some email messages, I found out he was working in the health care industry and now living in the Caribbean. As chance would have it, he was in Toronto on business for a few days. After some hastily typed notes, I discovered he would be returning home in a few hours. He agreed to meet me over coffee. I arrived early and was standing inside the coffee shop looking out the window in the direction I anticipated he would come. I wondered if I would recognize him after thirty-four years. I watched the sidewalk in the distance, scrutinizing each man as they walked toward me. Bruce could be any one of them, I thought. Whoever turned to walk into the coffee shop would narrow the field. Then I spotted him in the distance. He was taller and a little broader, but his long, slow, easy stride was unmistakable — a lot about us can change as we age, but I find that our gait is almost like a fingerprint. I pushed through the glass door to walk outside and head in his direction. I was smiling as I watched him approach. He must have seen me, because his face burst into a wide grin. His stride lengthened but did not quicken.

After the initial handshakes and pleasantries, we talked a bit about our families and what we were doing now. The conversation dwindled and became stilted and laboured as I sipped my coffee and he his juice as we searched for things to say to one another. We had come to the inevitable part where someone had to bring up the past. We spoke about those we remembered from '74 and the two other years we had spent together as cadets and then as NCOs. I tried to ask him a few questions about the day of the explosion, but he carefully and good-naturedly ducked them.

"Oh, that was so long ago," he said with a wave of his hand. Then his face changed: the corners of his mouth flattened out and his eyes narrowed. "So long ago," he breathed, looking away. I could see he was uncomfortable. There was no way I wanted to press him. It was difficult for me even to watch the transformation in him. I changed the subject to ease the tension, and we talked about his work for a while longer. Then he had to go. Before he left, he turned and abruptly said, "What did they expect us to do? We were just kids."

I got a note from one who was more obviously wrestling with his memories. He had just joined the private Web page and had sent me a private email on July 24, 2008. He couldn't understand how the explosion could have occurred. He further explained that he had continued on in the military. With his military knowledge and background, he failed to understand how an active grenade could end up with dummy training aids. It made no sense to him how an explosives expert would not see a live grenade mixed in with blue dummy training grenades.

I had no answer for him. Even if I explained the sequence of events that ultimately led to the explosion as I had found them in the inquest reports, it would not have made it any easier to understand, nor would it have altered the outcome. After thirty-four years it was evident that I wasn't the only one with unanswered questions. I had searched out some of the answers, though.

Some of us were plagued by horrible nightmares. One had been fighting with the Department of Veterans Affairs for years in an effort to receive treatment for his diagnosis of post-traumatic stress disorder. Although the diagnosis was directly related to the summer of 1974, the Veterans Affairs' response to him had been that, officially, cadets are not members of the Canadian Armed Forces, and so were not entitled to support for treatment. He said he had been depressed when he received the decision and was very glad to hear from Charles when he did. The renewed contact with us and news of the approaching reunion were exciting for him, at first.

He sent old pictures and greetings to many of us and brought up funny memories that we had forgotten. Soon, though, the tone of his email changed. The idea of meeting us all again dredged up his old demons, too. He started with descriptions of the things he had seen on the day of the explosion, but went into too much detail. He began railing against the government's treatment of the ex-cadets and describing his own frequent and sudden outbursts of anger, as well as the nightmares he was having. The nightmares were violent and his descriptions of them graphic. He also began hotly to dispute some of the recollections of others. Eventually, the notes became bitter and vitriolic, with the text sometimes written all in upper case without punctuation other than a series of exclamation points at the end.

Then, suddenly, as if a switch had been turned on, his tone changed. He sent a general note telling us he was severing contact. His battle with the government and the looming anniversary of the explosion, combined with the stress of possibly meeting some of us again, had contributed to a breakdown. The contrast between this final message to the group and the last few we had had from him was unsettling. It was like a calm period after a storm, when the sun shines to reveal destruction and debris. I could tell he had spent a considerable amount of time preparing the note. He sounded reasonable and articulate as he described an angry scene in his kitchen a few days before, when he had stood raving at his family and threatening to leave the country. When the dust had settled, he and his wife determined that it was the renewed association with us that had drawn him to the edge.

"The contacts I have had with many of you in the last little while have opened up a wound I am so desperately trying to heal," he wrote on June 23, 2008. "I am extremely vulnerable and if I were to continue, I know that I would lose my wife and kids. Be good to each other. Take time to heal." He was gone. We were cut off.

"We have to respect his wish and leave him for a while," said Charles the next time I heard from him. "I, alone, will be in touch with him periodically," he added, "just to maintain a minimal amount of contact." Charles thought that he might, one day, want to come back to the group, so he wanted to leave a pathway back to us if he needed it.

A note from another D Company member began with, "Hi Sarge." That stung. No one had ever called me "Sarge." I would have hotly

discouraged that. I had found him through the Internet and then sent
a note some time ago. I had started to give up hope of ever hearing
from him. He apologized for taking so long to respond. It wasn't easy
for him, he said, to get to the point of even answering my note.

He let me know he had been plagued by guilt and shame for years.
He had been badly injured in the explosion and had been unable
to move on that day. He had felt guilty about having been unable
to help his friends when they needed him. After many years, he had
finally learned to put those feelings aside so that the memory of July
30 didn't consume his daily life. His mirror, he said, presented him
with a reminder of the explosion every day, but he had learned to move
forward and keep his emotions securely tethered. The tethers had
come loose when we found him, he said. Charles had emailed him to
say he would contact him by phone. He admitted he had dreaded the
call, but had found it easier to talk to Charles than he had thought it
would be.

"So now, I think about it every day," he wrote to me on August
25, 2008. He had gone in search of his scrapbook and a diary of that
day. He commended us for trying to bring a reunion together. He
thought it might possibly be therapeutic and perhaps bring closure
for some. "Perhaps I will get to that point but I'm not there yet," he
said, suggesting that he would not be at the reunion. He couldn't see
how he could face his old friends and apologize for not being able to
help them. Like so many of us, he had kept the story to himself. He
didn't think anyone but those who had been there would understand.
And like the rest of us, he had not had contact with anyone from that
summer, until now.

Because of his injuries, he had spent quite some time in the hospital
and then been sent home on medical leave. He never did have a chance
to be with the platoon again, or even to say goodbye. He felt that had
added to his feelings of shame. "It's hard to believe that the boys from
our platoon are in their fifties," he wrote. "They are still fifteen- and
sixteen-year-olds to me."

I wrote back to him to let him know that he wasn't alone, that all of the boys I talked to shared the same feelings. What had happened to us, we kept to ourselves. Although it was a part of our identity, it was our secret identity. "I never really appreciated the term bittersweet," I told him in an email the next day, August 26, "until I heard from Charles and had to respond to my old friends with my hands shaking and my eyes watering."

Through some detective work, I was finally able to locate my old friend Paul Wheeler. I decided I would take a direct approach and tell him in an email about how Charles had contacted me and about the coming reunion. Much to my surprise, he answered quickly. His response was warm and receptive to meeting again, although he wouldn't be able to make it to the upcoming reunion, as he had already made his plans for the next few months. His feelings mirrored mine and so many of the others I had contacted. We traded several messages, caught up on what life had given us in the thirty-four years, and promised to maintain contact.

The group registered on the site had grown to more than forty, and we were eagerly exchanging email addresses and greetings. Many included the whole group in the conversations, while others who didn't wish to be identified or join the site or perhaps did not have access to the Internet contacted only Charles.

We were spread out across Canada, the United States, and even the Caribbean. In a strange coincidence, two fellows had worked together for close to ten years, unaware they had both been D Company members and in the barrack during the explosion. Charles had discovered it when he received their work mailing addresses and brought it to their attention. I think Charles was as amazed as they were when they found out.

Among the old photos posted on the Web site were pictures of smiles and some of the barracks, and images of boys standing at attention or laughing. There were new pictures, too, of people meeting for the first time after so many years. Someone also posted photos of five of the boys who had died. The pictures were yellow and faded, and the first one I saw rent my heart. His face had been etched in my memory as though carved in stone since that day at the hospital when I failed to identify him. I had no idea who he was until the moment I saw the picture with his name beneath it: Yves Langlois.

There was, however, no discussion of the past on the Web site itself. It was eerie how we had all come together and registered, but no one said a word about what had drawn us together in the first place. It was as if, publicly, we all wanted to continue a silent association with one another. Perhaps it would be different at the reunion in the coming July.

I wasn't to find out. As it turned out, I couldn't go despite my best intentions. After I had wrestled with my feelings and had made the difficult decision to be there, the people in charge of the memorial parade at CFB Valcartier decided to change the date to coincide with a regimental anniversary being held a few days earlier, making it impossible for me and many of the others to modify our plans. The effect of this was twofold. It prevented some of us from attending, and by tucking it into a larger celebration, it seemed to trivialize the memorial by making it a mere footnote to the larger and more colourful carnival atmosphere of the regimental anniversary. It appeared to me that they were trying to hide this tiny bitter pill within a spoonful of honey.

After the date of the memorial parade had come and gone, Charles Gutta called me. He had attended the memorial parade and had met a handful of others from 1974 who had been able to rearrange their schedules. But he wasn't happy.

"I am writing an after-action report, so all of our members will know what is going on and how we were treated. We'll post it on the site," he said, making reference to the private Web page. He let me know it had been a disappointing situation and very uncomfortable for the attendees. The base administration originally had led Charles to believe not only that he and his group were welcome, but that they would be guests at the officers' mess for lunch after the parade. As it turned out, the camp was completely unprepared for them. They told Charles there wasn't enough food for them, and he felt their lack of hospitality had bordered on contempt. "It was over thirty degrees outside and we were standing on the asphalt parade square," he said. "We couldn't even get a drink of water. It was embarrassing."

He let me know that, a few days after the memorial parade, he had met with the people in charge at his request—specifically, the regional director. He expressed his displeasure at the date change with so little notice, that people had made plans to be there on the original date and that travel arrangements and hotel reservations had been made and then had to be cancelled. The director merely responded that he had not been concerned about changing the date and assumed that he would not be inconveniencing anyone. He also told Charles that the veteran cadets had been invited to all the previous memorial parades, and each time they had been a no-show.

"Wait a minute," I said, interrupting Charles. I was shocked to hear this. "I have never been invited," I told him. "I never even knew about it. How could they possibly invite us? They couldn't have even found us!"

"You're getting emotional," he cautioned sharply. "Calm yourself." Then he sighed. From his perspective, the director had made it clear that having the ex-cadets at the memorial parade wasn't important to them.

"But I told him," said Charles, "this is an important event for these people. There are over one hundred and thirty people that were directly affected by this incident. Some of them were injured and their friends were killed. A number of them wanted to be there!" Charles was also getting increasingly emotional as he related the story to me. He caught himself and apologized.

There is nothing worse than feeling like an unwanted guest. It is humiliating and degrading. Although he didn't say it, I felt that Charles wasn't embarrassed for himself as much as for the people he had taken with him. The base had been his regimental home for years, and I believe he was mortified that the administration had shown its guests such deplorable hospitality. Then, without apology, he tried to justify it by saying that even though the guests had been invited, they were not welcome. It became clear to me as Charles and I spoke that, despite the pomp and pageantry of the memorial parade they put on every summer, it was all for show and had no substance. The meaning and significance of the memorial had long ago been lost. The parade itself was now just an interruption of their schedule, and having guests meant a responsibility to act as hosts, a role they were loath to take on.

They weren't interested in the reason for the memorial. The parade was a requirement, as I discovered, when in one of my searches for information, my search terms took me to the standing orders for the cadet camp. The document was titled "Centre d'instruction d'été des cadets de l'armée—Valcartier céremonie du souvenir, Ordre Permanent 561." The protocol, commands, and drill movements were blueprinted, from the march onto the parade square to the removal of the berets for the moment of silence, but the parade was an inconvenience and having us there would be a nuisance.

"Do you want to know what he told me?" Charles paused. "He said," he paused again. "He said, 'That was thirty-four years ago. It is over. We have turned the page.'"

There was silence again on the other end of the phone.

"They ignored us in '74," Charles said quietly, "and they're dismissing us now."

I could never go back.

And yet, I think of my brave friends almost every day: of Fullum bent over to cut off a bloody boot with a knife; Medvescek running to help with stretchers and applying dressings; Slater in the barrack; Banzal, who beat me to the medical inspection room; Seguin and Gibeault and their grim faces as they were going in to identify the bodies; Sergeant Gutta calling the roll in the mess without giving anything away; Snopek trying to shield me from the bloody putties in the mess; and Wheeler in the barrack with his face shrouded in the powder smoke, bent over an injured boy. These are only the ones I can remember seeing. Others worked the same way, running with stretchers and doing what had to be done, but out of my sight. They understood their responsibilities, knew the limits of their capabilities, and pushed beyond them to ensure their friends were brought to care and safety. These were my brave friends.

•

My family and I attend the Canada Day parade every year in our small town, and everyone who lines the street to watch tries to dress in something that is red and white. The result is a group of people who embody our flag while they celebrate the country's birthday. We stand on the main street, watching the floats cobbled together by local merchants, associations, schools, churches, and service clubs drift down the street accompanied by the occasional decorated bicycle or costumed dog and a sprinkling of bands. The bands all seem to be playing "The Maple Leaf Forever" as they pass us.

In the middle somewhere, following their colours, march the members of the local Legion in their grey pants, navy blazers, and berets, wearing their decorations. Their numbers are fewer each year, but those still on parade walk with their heads held high. I feel an affinity with the members of the Legion because, when I was a cadet, I had the opportunity to march with the Legion members on November 11 each year on the way to the cenotaph or a Remembrance Day service. When we marched together, less than thirty years had passed since the Second World War, and many of the veterans were not much older than I am now. I always make a point of being on my feet as they approach, and I applaud as they pass.

In late October every year, I like to buy a poppy for Remembrance Day from one of the veterans, although that is getting increasingly difficult as there are fewer of them around. To help out, the cadets in my town sell poppies for the local Legion, but I never buy one from them. I tell myself that I prefer to buy a poppy from a Legion member, and that is true. But it is also true that I can't bear to speak to the cadets. I can see them standing out in front of the grocery stores and liquor stores as I approach. They stand tall in their shined boots and pressed uniforms, with trays of poppies. That is when I look for alternative entrances. If all the entrances are covered, I often head to another store. It has nothing to do with the cadets, but sometimes I can't even bear to make eye contact with them.

Afterword

I had been in regular contact with Charles Gutta, my ex-company sergeant major. Our discussions were usually around his plans for another reunion and how he was searching out additional members of the company who still eluded him. So I was more than a little surprised when he blindsided me in September 2009 with, "You need help. When are you going to get it?"

"What do you mean?" I asked, knowing full well what he meant, but hoping he would be too discreet to elaborate. Charles wasn't known to be anything less than direct, though. He came back at me as if I should be chastised.

"Come on," he said. "Don't be difficult. You have PTSD and you need help." He was talking about post-traumatic stress disorder, a severe anxiety disorder that can occur after a physical or psychological trauma or a combination of both. Although I had heard of PTSD in the past, I had never connected it with myself. The traumas I had been involved with were too long ago to have had any impact on my life, I thought. I was fine.

"You are not alone, you know," Charles persisted. "I am getting help and so are a few of the others."

"It was over thirty years ago," I answered breezily over the phone, trying to shut down the conversation. "I'm fine."

"You're not fine and you're no expert on the subject. Don't take my word for it," Charles said. "Go see your family doctor and explain what happened in '74. That's all you have to do."

"All right," I said, to stop his badgering, "I'll call my doctor."

I didn't call my doctor though. I needed to think about it a bit more, quite a bit more. What Charles had said continued to nag at me. I had recently read a book by a high-ranking soldier who had been on a peacekeeping mission. Lieutenant-General Roméo Dallaire had witnessed monstrous atrocities in Rwanda during his tour of duty. The book also contained an account of his battle with PTSD. Even though I recognized General Dallaire's symptoms as similar to my own, I again dismissed PTSD in my own case. His circumstances were completely different. He had been a career soldier and what he witnessed was in a war zone. My experience, on the other hand, had been as an eighteen-year-old at a summer camp for cadets. It couldn't even compare to what he had witnessed, and it was over thirty years ago.

But Charles's request rankled, and I began to suspect that he was right — I might be suffering from PTSD. Knowing that the next time he and I would be in contact he would ask me for a progress report, I finally gave in and made an appointment with my doctor. I was sure it would be a waste of time. I would let the doctor know matter-of-factly that someone suggested that I be assessed for PTSD.

When I saw her, she simply asked me why someone would suggest that I be assessed. Other than my wife and one or two others, I had never spoken of it to anyone. If on a rare occasion anyone would ask, I always deflected the conversation away to another topic. There was no escaping it this time, though. This was the sole reason I was talking to the doctor. As soon as I opened my mouth to tell her why, I no longer had any doubt that Charles was right. What was to be my brief and glib explanation was hijacked by a flood of emotion that I could not contain.

She referred me to a PTSD specialist for a full assessment. Again, though, I was sceptical. Why would I want to relive the trauma of over thirty years ago? What purpose could it possibly serve to rehash the pain by telling the story to a total stranger who took notes and nodded sagely? My previous exposure to therapy was the warped version perpetuated by Hollywood. What I would quickly learn, however, was that there is real help for those suffering with PTSD. The treatment doesn't erase the tragedy; it just moves the old traumas away from a part of the brain where they constantly create a sense of urgency and panic to where they become benign memories.

Too many of us are under the impression that we must endure the disorder unaided and in silence. There is a feeling that we must be strong and show no weakness for our family's sake, or to support the image of ourselves we feel we must present to the world. But that can be a selfish notion, because it is not only we who suffer the effects of our trauma — our families bear the burden of our symptoms, too. They suffer our sleepless nights with us, as well as our nightmares, flashbacks, hypervigilance, outbursts of anger, and all the other related symptoms that join together to keep us chained to the trauma that has come to torment and enslave us. If we choose to refuse to take the path toward healing, our friends who shared the trauma with us suffer as well, because when we deny our own symptoms we also deny theirs. By hiding behind bravado and denial, we risk impeding their healing. Once I was better informed, I came to know that it was my duty to my family, to the other survivors, and to their families, to seek treatment for my PTSD.

"Thanks," I said to Charles over the phone. "I went to see my doctor. It will take some time, but things are already going very well."

"Good," he said. "Now, let's see if we can get some help for a few more."

Notes

Can You Attend?

1. "Two killed in crash of Snowbird plane," *Toronto Star*, October 9, 2008.

2. Department of National Defence, Assistant Deputy Minister (Finance and Corporate Services), Director of Access to Information and Privacy; available online at http://www.admfincs.forces.gc.ca/aip/cr-dc-06-eng. asp.

3. A0192142 Military Police Report (September 19, 1974), page 3, para. 5.

Lecture Preparations

4. A0192143 Military Police Report (September 19, 1974), page 16, para. 92.

5. Ibid., page 19, para. 93.

6. Ibid., page 36, para. 107.

7. Ibid.

8. Ibid.

9. A0192144 Military Police Report (September 19, 1974), page 2, para. 111.

10. Ibid.

11. A0192143, page 34, para. 106.

12. A0192144, page 8, para. 120.

13. A0192143, page 34, para. 106.

14. A0192144, page 2, para. 111.

15. A0192143, page 26, para. 102.

16.   A0192144, page 12, para. 125 J.

17.   A0192143, page 37, para. 107.

18.   Ibid., page 28, para. 102.

19.   Ibid., page 37, para. 107.

20.   A0192144, page 15, para. 125 P.

21.   A0192143, page 27, para. 102.

22.   Ibid., page 25, para. 101.

23.   There might be some confusion as to how many live grenades were in circulation in the lecture. This passage is just one among the witness statements in which the number is vague. In this instance, there are even two different types of grenades, the M-36 and the M-61, which look quite different. In another, the witness reports that an ammunition technician replaced the grenades in the cardboard box but not in the containers that were used to transport live grenades. This suggests multiple containers were in the box of dummies.

24.   A0192143, page 16, para. 92.

25.   Ibid., page 38, para. 107.

26.   Ibid.

27.   Ibid., page 32, para. 105.

28.   Ibid.

29.   Ibid., page 38, para. 107.

30.   Ibid.

Pre-inspection

31.   Department of National Defence, Canadian Forces Enrolment Form (Ottawa), section 4, para. 1.

Safety Lecture

32.   A0192143, page 16, para. 91.

33.   A0192142, page 18, para. 29.

34.   A0192144, page 14, para. 125 O.

35.   A0192142, page 18, para. 29.

36.   A0192144, page 14, para. 125 N.

37. A0192143, page 19, para. 92.

38. Ibid. page 14, para. 89.

39. Ibid., page 13, para. 88.

40. Ibid., page 14, para. 89.

The Days After

41. A0192141 Military Police Report (September 19, 1974), page 10, para. 4.

42. A0192154 Military Police Report (September 19, 1974), page 40.

Summer 1974 Closes

43. A0192155 Military Police Report (September 19, 1974), page 37.

Archival Discoveries

44. "6 cadets killed 32 others hurt in Quebec blast," *Toronto Star,* July 31, 1974, page 1.

45. "Grenade blast still a mystery coroner says," *Toronto Star,* October 24, 1974, page A9.

46. Ibid.

47. Ibid.

48. "Instructor blamed in grenade blast that killed 6 cadets," *Toronto Star,* March 12, 1975, page F14.

49. Ibid.

50. Ibid.

51. "Grenade case man denies charge," *Toronto Star,* April 23, 1975, page C14.

52. A0192171 Military Police Report, Inquest Report 5GC Valcartier (March 4, 1974), page 22.

53. Ibid., page 23.

54. "Quebec officer to stand trial in blast deaths," *Toronto Star,* May 21, 1976, page B6.

55. "Officer to stand trial for death of six cadets," *Lethbridge Herald,* May 21, 1976, page 36.

56.   "Instructor acquitted in deaths of cadets," *Lethbridge Herald*, June 22, 1977, page 40.

57.   Ibid.

58.   Ibid.

Acknowledgements

This book was a long journey and sometimes a difficult one. It could not have been brought to completion without the help and support of some talented and supportive people.

I would like to thank my editor, Paula Sarson, for her skill, sensitivity, patience, and delicate touch; Susanne Alexander, Colleen Kitts, and the entire team at Goose Lane Editions for their support and encouragement throughout the process and, of course, for inviting me into their flock; Julie Scriver for giving the story an outstanding look on the covers and between them; my copy editor Barry Norris; my wife Angie, the angel on my shoulder who makes such a profound impact on everything I do; my wonderful agent Daphne Hart of the Helen Heller Agency; Colin Caldwell, for initiating contact with all the survivors; and Andrew Halfnight and Robert Smol, who thought the story was worth telling. My sincere thanks to my friend Charles Gutta, whose rock solid support and wisdom have inspired not only me but all those who know him.

And a special thank you to Barbara Anscheutz for helping me to walk through it all again without stumbling.

•

The following passages include quoted dialogue for which permission has been obtained:

Quoted by permission of Aleth Bruce:

pp. 173-174: "After the initial...We were just kids.'"

Quoted by permission:

p. 175: "Then, suddenly, as if...We were cut off."

Bibliography

Department of National Defence, Canadian Forces Enrolment Form. Ottawa.

Lethbridge Herald. "Blast kills cadets," July 31, 1974, page 1.

_____. "Instructor acquitted in deaths of cadets," June 22, 1977, page 40.

_____. "Officer to stand trial for death of six cadets," May 21, 1976, page 36.

_____. "Two men die when shell explodes on target range," May 11, 1977, page 2.

_____. "Valcartier explosion," August 1, 1974, page 2.

Military Police. Investigation Case File # DS 025-20-74, received under the Access to Information Act.

New York Times. "6 Cadets killed in Quebec," August 1, 1974.

Toronto Star. "6 cadets killed 32 others hurt in Quebec blast," July 31, 1974, page 1.

_____. "Blast-injured cadet becomes sergeant," November 12, 1974, page A14.

_____. "Bravery of cadets in blast honoured," August 20, 1974, page A7.

_____. "Grenade blast still a mystery coroner says," October 24, 1974, page A9.

_____. "Grenade case man denies charge," April 23, 1975, page C14.

_____. "Instructor blamed in grenade blast that killed 6 cadets," March 12, 1975, page F14.

_____. "Quebec officer to stand trial in blast deaths," May 21, 1976, page B6.

_____. "Two killed in crash of Snowbird plane," October 9, 2008.

Index